AF559579

A FULL LIFE

A FULL LIFE

SABIRA MERCHANT

with Mitali Parekh

Foreword by Alyque Padamsee

Preface by Lara Dutta

JAICO PUBLISHING HOUSE

Ahmedabad Bangalore Bhopal Chennai
Delhi Hyderabad Kolkata Lucknow Mumbai

Published by Jaico Publishing House
A-2 Jash Chambers, 7-A Sir Phirozshah Mehta Road
Fort, Mumbai - 400 001
jaicopub@jaicobooks.com
www.jaicobooks.com

A FULL LIFE
ISBN 978-93-90166-86-2

First Jaico Impression: 2022

Page design and layout: R. Ajith Kumar, Delhi

Printed by
Nutech Photolithographers, New Delhi

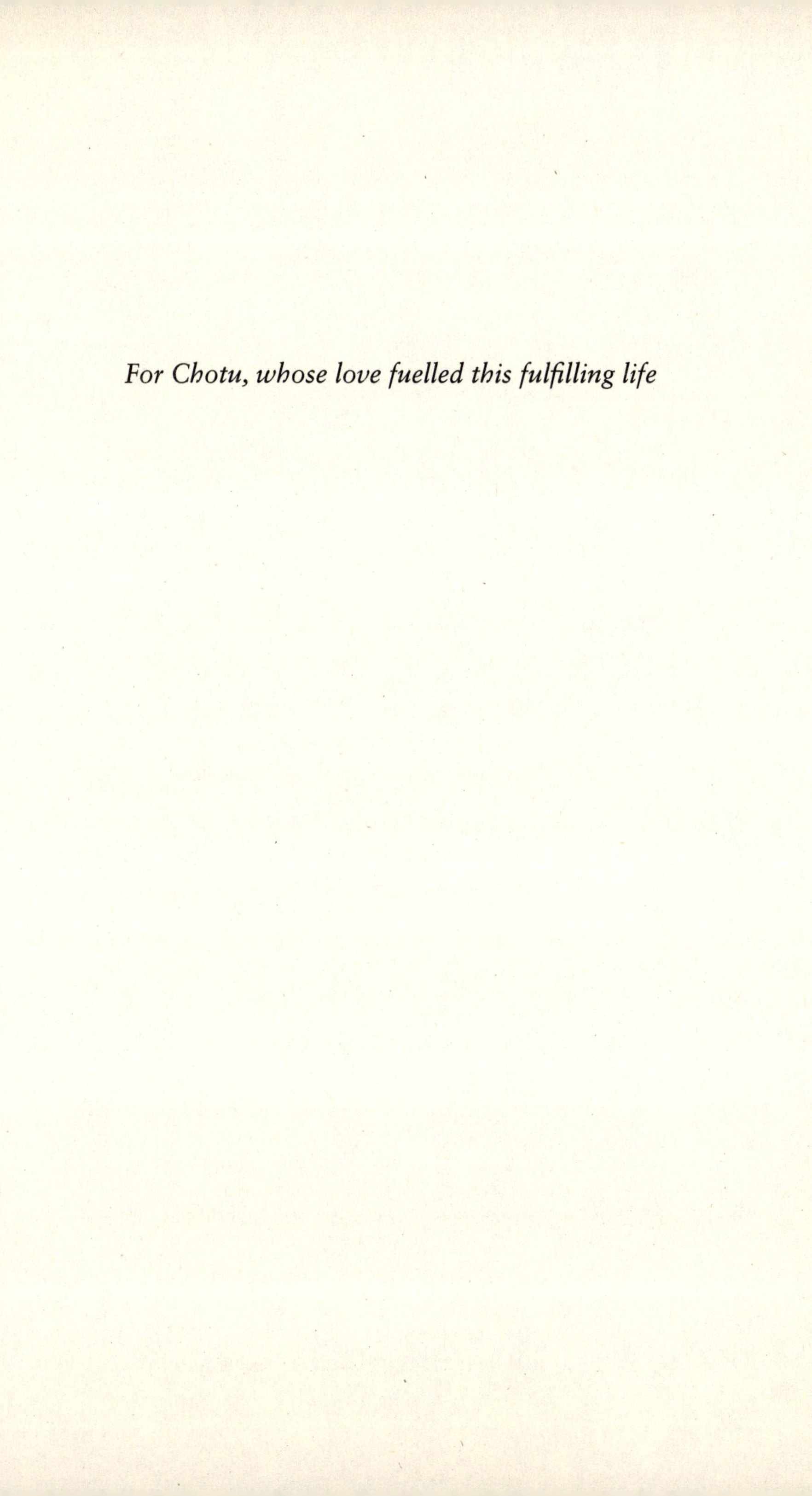

For Chotu, whose love fuelled this fulfilling life

Contents

Foreword

SABIRA IS A TRUE drama queen.

I first met her through my wife Pearl, whom she had approached for a role in theatre.

Sabira said, "Well, I have never acted, but I would like to act; I would be willing to do anything in the theatre."

Now that is something I love to hear, and I was impressed with her enthusiasm. Pearl took her under her wing to do the costumes for *Hamlet*. It was a play of formidable proportions. There must have been easily a hundred costumes. I had no time to go backstage and be nice to people as I was trying to get this Shakespeare play off the ground.

Pearl said, "Don't worry about anything. Sabira is in charge; she's well-organized, very disciplined... and she makes lists." When I heard that, my heart leapt. I fell in love with her at that moment because I am the greatest list-maker of all time.

Sabi, as we called her, was very keen on talking to actors, making them feel at home and seeing that at every interval, they got proper tea and biscuits.

Then, the next play came around. It was called *The Word*, written by Pat (Partap) Sharma, who was a fledgling playwright at the time. It wasn't a great play, but it was an unusual play. I liked the idea because it was set in a fallout shelter.

We are talking about the '60s, and at that time, there was a lot of fear in the world about the atom bomb and how at any minute it could fall anywhere.

I had the good fortune to find an under-construction venue. The Government Dental College was building an underground theatre and they hadn't put any seats in yet. A friend of mine and Chotu—Sabira's husband—provided wooden crates that the audience sat on.

The shelter was run by a woman called Ma, and the others were all symbolic characters. There was one character, which I could not cast: a schoolgirl. Most girls were in school anyway, so how to get them for rehearsals?

Pearl says to me, "You know, Sabira looks like a little girl. And would you believe she has three children?"

I asked her, "Would you be willing to do it?"

"I would like to try," said Sabira.

So I put her in a uniform with a sash, and we started rehearsals. This underground shelter could only be accessed by a rope ladder coming from the ceiling and everyone had to practise coming down from it. It's very difficult because it swings, you see. But Sabira was a great sport and she came down.

Unfortunately, one day, Chotu came to a rehearsal and saw his wife climbing down a rope ladder.

"She can't do that," he said.

"Why not?" I asked.

"She's quite capable; I have seen her."

"But..." he said, and he couldn't say the word 'panties', "You can see her knickers!"

"Oh yeah," I said, "I never thought of that." Pearl, as usual, rushed to the rescue and said, "Don't worry, I'll put her in bloomers held by elastic at the knee."

Sabira was good in the play. I wouldn't say she was brilliant, because she wasn't. We finally came to a very challenging play, *A Streetcar Named Desire*, which I had always wanted to do. I had seen the movie with Marlon Brando and Vivien Leigh, for which Leigh won the Academy Award.

Pearl and I put our heads together and said, "Okay, there is only one person we can choose for Vivien Leigh's part, and that is Sabira Merchant." And for Marlon Brando's part, a young man had come to me from St. Paul's in Darjeeling. He was a well-built guy called Dalip Tahil.

Sabira and I sat down to tackle these roles. It called for the leading actress to have a Southern American drawl. Not too much, but enough to give that effete, old-world charm.

One of the great lines in the play, which I quote very often and so does Sabira is, "I have always relied on the kindness of strangers." It's a very touching line. It comes after Brando's character rapes Leigh's Blanche in a drunken rage. It's a terrifying scene, and after that Blanche goes half off her rocker. Slowly, she becomes totally dissociated from reality. They phone up the doctor who says she now has to be committed to a home. I played the doctor and it was a one-line role. She says, "Who are you?" "I have come to take care of you," I say, and offer my arm like a typical Southern gentleman. She puts her hand on my arm and says, "I have always relied on the kindness of strangers."

This was in the '70s and the play ran for 50 shows all around India. Everybody wanted to see Sabira Merchant in *A Streetcar Named Desire*.

Sabira was of course very young and very beautiful, but as soon as she appeared on stage, you could see she had one of the things great actresses, not good actresses, have—a touch of vulnerability. You felt that this character could get hurt, and the audience's heart goes out to her. Meryl Streep has this quality, and I would compare Sabira to her. In every play she has done with me, she has that quality.

The second thing about Sabira is that she's very disciplined. She was very young when she joined the theatre and young actors think theatre is fun. They come to rehearsals to fool around with the cast. But Sabira would sit in a corner and study her lines.

Improvisation is a great thing, but only in rehearsal. To try and discover your character. Once you have set the character, you must stick to the lines. Because if you go off them and your improvisation quality fails you, the nervousness shows. You don't know what to say. The actors call it 'drying up'.

But Sabira never does. In fact, she is so good that occasionally, when the other actor misses a cue, she will prompt that person on stage with her back to the audience.

This is very helpful to newcomers. She recently did a play for me called *Legends of Lovers* and my youngest daughter, Shazahn, was on stage for the first time. Sabira was an enormous help to her—she sat with her, went through her lines, told her to be confident and not worry about a thing.

I have been a bit ill recently and she has been very particular about ringing me up every day, inquiring about my health and whether I have taken the medicines she suggested. Once I asked her, "How do you manage theatre?"

For a good part of her senior life, she was looking after Chotu. "It's my relief," she said, "I get away from home problems by becoming someone else."

She really has all the makings of a theatre great—discipline, vulnerability and excellent speech.

We have done about 10 plays together, and she has also grown incrementally with each role. I could see that she was enjoying expanding her capability to play different people.

I did *Tughlaq* in 1970, which was the first Indian play to have people queuing up outside the theatre. She played Tughlaq's (Kabir Bedi) stepmother, the senior queen, who falls in love with him.

Sabira played a mature woman excellently and it was very interesting to see the interaction between her and Kabir who made his name in that one play and was snapped up by the movies. He was innocent with no idea of her attraction, while she emanated sexual heat.

Then, there was *Death of a Salesman* in 1981. Sabira played Linda Loman, the wife of the main character, and it was the opposite of Blanche Dubois. Linda was always quiet, always subdued and bullied by her husband, Willy Loman, played by me. She has two or three beautiful scenes about why she loves her husband, even though he is oppressive and a failure. The final scene, which is set in the graveyard after Willy commits suicide, is only about five minutes long but Sabira was riveting in it. At every show, she brought the audience to tears.

Sabira has got a terrific ability in tragedy, and she is good at comedy also because her diction is excellent. In comedy, your diction must be perfect.

In 1990's *Othello*, Sabira was back on stage with Kabir Bedi. She played Emilia, Desdemona's maid. In the end, when she sees Desdemona on stage, she was able to show heightened emotion without screaming or shouting.

She played a small but powerful role in my 2006's *Macbeth* too, that of Lady McDuff.

Sabira is no doubt my favourite actor, not just actress. She has this ability to become the role, not just play it. And she likes a challenge. We are doing a play together right now in which she plays Julius Caesar. And never did she think she could not play Caesar. Most actresses will say, "Caesar? How can I play Caesar?" Sabira will just say, "Wow. I'd like to try that."

As a friend, you will rarely meet a character like Sabira. She is a warm and helpful person, and a gracious, smiling host. Her charm is persuasive.

She somehow cajoled the Muslim owners of a building to allow dancing and drinking in their premises at Studio 29. Her brilliant idea there was a room next to the dance floor, where people tired of dancing would just sit on the carpet and have a drink and chat and smoke. The atmosphere there was literally like a house party.

If I was tired after a hard day, and didn't want to dance, I would go sit in that room. The people you met there were not just flibbertigibbets. It was a mixed bag of older people who spoke about the social missions of India, and the younger lot who would talk about the latest music. It was a nice eclectic mix and Sabira was the spirit of the place. We were all heartbroken when Studio 29 shut down.

The discotheque could have also been a hub for the arts. We did a few readings there and Sabira was thinking of hanging paintings to make it a modern art space. It was a young people's cultural centre; not stiff-shirted like the Taj [the Taj Mahal hotel].

I don't think Chotu liked the idea of his wife running a disco. He was Muslim and came from a well-honoured family, so I think these things were aberrations. But he loved Sabira enormously, so he supported her.

It was a very interesting marriage. He was not involved in her theatre life at all. He was a businessman and none of her three children were interested in the arts either.

So, she had a lonely part to play, but to her, the theatre was another family.

Alyque Padamsee
Adman and theatre personality
Breach Candy, 2017

Preface

IN DECEMBER OF 1999, I took a decision that would forever impact my life. After being pursued for a long time by the Times of India Group to participate in the Femina Miss India pageant, I finally took the plunge. Leading up to the Miss India 2000 contest, we embarked on a rigorous training programme that was geared towards refining us as candidates who could represent the country impeccably on an international stage.

I vividly remember meeting Sabira for the very first time. Exhausted from being up since the crack of dawn, and having been put through a demanding physical fitness regime with little more than a lime shot in our bellies, with our heads crammed full of art, music and culture appreciation jargon and sore, blistered feet from hours of training to walk in heels, our motley bunch of aspiring contestants looked more like malnourished street urchins than future beauty queens. Into the hall of these wide-eyed novices marched a diminutive but extremely powerful dynamo.

Through all the years that I have known Sabira, she has remained exactly as she was that first time I encountered her. She is always calm, unruffled and inordinately elegant and yet exudes an energy that one can sense nestled within her like a tightly-coiled spring. It took her hardly 15 minutes to assess the whole room. She knew exactly which girl needed her diction to be polished, which one required her vocabulary to be enhanced, who needed to build confidence to express an individual thought and who was clearly quite hopeless!

I've said it over the last 17 years and I will say it again. Very simply, there is no one in this country quite like Sabira Merchant. She is irreplaceable. Her experience combined with very effective training techniques and her patience, diligence and complete understanding of the requirements of her clients make her THE go-to person to transform your personality forever.

May 12, 2000 gave India its second Miss Universe and I believe that my individual score of 9.99 has been the highest ranking in history. None of that would have been possible without the guidance and support of Sabira, whom I still look upon as a mentor, guide and my ultimate inspiration. What an honour and privilege it is to have known you, Sabira! And if in my lifetime I can be half the lady you are, I would consider it a life accomplished. God bless.

Lara Dutta-Bhupathi

Actor, entrepreneur and the winner of the
Miss Universe 2000 pageant

Prologue

My Blessed Life

THE IDEA FOR THIS autobiography germinated in 2016 when one of the professionals who helps me organize my Corporate Finesse workshops suggested a self-help handbook for those seeking to polish their diction and etiquette. It would be something that would encapsulate the work I do with corporates and the Miss India contestants.

As I pondered on this, I realized that the lessons I have been passing on were what I had the privilege to be exposed to all through my life. My love for words and determination to teach myself how to pronounce them correctly came in school. An ease among strangers was instilled in my formative years by my father. I even learnt to straddle the two different cultures of Bandra and Karachi because I knew how to be at home with anyone I met.

The fire to better myself was stoked by my fiancé who sent me to Europe to see the world outside Bombay before I settled into matrimony as a mere teenager. And then I was able to observe the decorum followed by the refined folks of South Bombay through my association with Lady Soonu Jeejeebhoy, Soonu Godrej and their elite philanthropic groups.

A lesson on diction and words would not be as interesting, I thought, without a peek into television and radio, and all the English programming we did in these mediums under the captainship of Adi Marzban.

Even today, the young men and women who attend my workshops in the far corners of the country are sent there by parents who grew up watching *What's the Good Word* on TV. Or, they have seen Lara Dutta and Priyanka Chopra articulate their dreams and win international beauty crowns. Perhaps their parents met while dancing at Studio 29 which was more a cultural juggernaut than just another disco.

It occurred to me that how friends and social acquaintances helped a teen bride from Bandra blossom into a young mother and then a *memsahib* might be an arresting read. It would also be interesting to write about how I made my way through the world using diplomacy, a currency that has never dropped in value.

For the younger reader, I wanted to paint a picture of a mellower, more social South Bombay before it became the driven, busy corporate creature of today. I wanted to look back to a time when socializing meant potluck with friends, an evening at the theatre, or to jive to a live band. When enrichment came not from objects but from people.

I wanted to share the honour and memories of being

directed by Alyque and Pearl Padamsee, of what it was like to see SH Raza and MF Husain sipping tea at the Samovar, and be bewitched by the Kendalls performing at your school. You'd just have to walk into a cafe in Kala Ghoda to meet some luminary who would widen your world.

All of this would not have been possible without the love and companionship of my husband Chotu who opened the world to me and pushed me at every step to expand my horizon. I grew up alongside my children Aly, Heena and Saleem who must have thought it normal to have such a busybody Mummy and tolerated all my hyperactivity.

The kind folk at Jaico Publishing House agreed that a self-help booklet would be dry and may not capture the richness of this life. Truth is, dear reader, I have been gifted a wonderful, fulfilling life. And I hope you enjoy reading about it as much as I enjoy living it.

Sabira Merchant

1

My Father's Daughter

"YOU KNOW, MUMMY-DADDY are not your real parents," my cousin Shama said to me as we played seven tiles on her balcony. "Your real parents didn't want you, that's why they gave you away."

I was about four or five years old when those words split my world into two.

What did she mean? My stylish, happy-go-lucky, doting, practical Daddy was not my father? That serious, conservative and religious couple that visited us sometimes were my real parents? Would I have to move to Pakistan with them?

As soon as Shama uttered those words, I ran to Daddy and asked him if it was true. He reassured me amply that though I was adopted, he loved me as much or even more than his own. And this remained the truth throughout our lives. Even as an adult, I only had to say, "Daddy, I need you", and his only and immediate response would be, "I'll be right there."

I was born on August 4, 1942 at Juliet D'sa nursing home on Girgaum Chowpatty to the man who was later known as the architect of Pakistan. I was Gulshan Thariani (née Vaziralli) and Abdul Hussain's fifth child. When my mother conceived, she promised her childless brother—Hazir 'Haaji' Hussain Vaziralli—that the baby she bore, be it a girl or a boy, would be his. As a result, the first phone call at my birth went out to Haaji to tell him he had been blessed with a daughter.

For nine months, I lived with my biological parents, Bapaji and Baima, in Mahim while my mother nursed me. After that I went home to Haaji-bhai and Khatija Vaziralli (née Chittiwala)—my Daddy and Mummy—at our family home in the small fishing village of Bandra.

Villa Vazir on Kane Road is still the home I recede into in my dreams. Every time I am ill or in need of comfort, the image of Villa Vazir comes to me and envelopes me in the love of my many cousins, aunts and uncles, and most importantly, my Daddy.

It was designed by my biological father, who was known as Bombay's Chawl King, for his wife's family. He built many landmarks in the city, some of which wove in and out of my life, guided by destiny's hand.

Back in the 1940s, the suburb was like a hill station—you knew where you were by the churches and their tolling bells. A hazy mist hung around the mornings and tiny fishing boats would moor at the beach. A fisherwoman would bring the freshest catch to our doorstep, which my mother would quickly fry up for breakfast. The inhabitants were a mix of Parsees, Christians, Anglo-Indians and Muslims.

Villa Vazir stood on Bandstand, behind what is now

superstar Shah Rukh Khan's iconic mansion Mannat. Right behind it was Mount Mary Church, and a short amble away was the rocky beach which I would head to with a little pail to collect shells, pebbles and sea glass as little crabs scurried about. The promenades and boundary walls that confine the beach now were to come much later. A part of Villa Vazir still exists, while a portion has given way to a high-rise.

One entered the home through the cantilevered veranda, held up by columns. Under the columns were two apartments, rented out to the Batras and the Tandons.

The heart of the home was the dining room, into which opened the other rooms. There were two bedrooms on either side with their private balconies, occupied by Aunty Noorjehan and Uncle Keki, and Uncle Yaseen and Aunty Abida and their families. Our room was at the back; there was also a spare room there where my aunts would stay when they visited.

The large kitchen, aided by a sizeable pantry, would be buzzing all day with food for this whole clan.

Over this bustling kingdom presided my grandmother, the formidable Fatima Vaziralli. Dadima had been widowed very early in life and brought up three daughters and five sons, educated all of them and found them suitable partners to marry. She had smooth, slim legs and excellent skin, which I luckily inherited.

This matriarch ran the home and the family businesses. Every week, she would put on her power suit—a black *gajji* silk *odhna* with a very fine *bandhani* and *gota* border draped over her *farack* (Indianization of the 'frock' which is a long maxi dress that reached till the ankles and had sleeves till the elbow), *ijjar*s (long, parallel pants), and a black velvet *potli* with an 'F' embroidered in gold—to do the accounts with the Mehtajis.

She would tally the rent collected from the various apartments and commercial buildings she owned and ensure the Mehtajis kept records. The family also ran a transport business, so for a very long time, she was the core breadwinner for our clan.

Once a week, Dadima enforced the dreaded 'Air India time'. All the little ones would have to line up to swallow a gruesome spoonful of castor oil which was considered a laxative and an all-round health tonic. No matter how much we tried to dodge or hide from this dreadful ritual, she would seek the errant grandchild out and ensured he or she had a spoonful.

Dadima remained a commanding presence right till the very end. At the ripe old age of 89, she became very ill. We all thought she was about to pass on and I went to the hospital with a white cloth to wrap her body in. Though in ill-health, she gripped my hand tightly, and to our surprise, not only recovered but even sprouted black hair. She passed away four or five years later.

"*Yeh mera tara hai* (She is my star)," was how she described me, because I was obedient and like her, disciplined with a strong sense of duty.

Like the *chawl*s Bapaji designed, Villa Vazir had many open spaces which we children—I lived with eight or nine cousins—spent our days in, playing cricket or seven tiles.

Among these cousins was Shama who told me about my parents.

This is why I always tell adoptive parents to find ways to tell their children the truth as early as possible. Tell them, "Because we loved you, we took you away."

As the Partition loomed, there were hushed conversations in our home about moving to Pakistan. Bapaji had been personally invited by Mohammed Ali Jinnah to help him build the new Islamic nation.

My biological father was also a poet, an artist and the editor of a newspaper called *Watan Daily*. He owned 18 properties in Mumbai, which he would have to give up to the government were he to go to Pakistan. Though I, his biological child, lived in India, he couldn't leave it all to me as there is no legal adoption in Islam.

Before leaving, he made many visits to Villa Vazir asking Daddy to let me go so I could be reunited with his family. At night, I would sneak out of bed to eavesdrop on these conversations and would be very worried about how I would adapt to a new country and a new set of parents and assimilate into a pack of six siblings.

"But my heart belongs to her now," Daddy told my parents. "You will break it if you take her away."

And so, I stayed on as Haaji-bhai's daughter. My parents had no intention of uprooting their lives. India was where their business, friends and families were, and they felt quite safe here.

Giving me away became a source of deep regret for Bapaji and Baima. Bapaji truly believed that it was his divine duty to inculcate the teachings of Islam in his offspring. Daddy was a westernized creature with a lot of Parsi influence, eating and drinking everything outside our home, and praying perfunctorily. He would go to the mosque only on holy days and copy the movements of those around him because frankly, he didn't know how to offer namaz.

Mummy conceived soon after I came to them and Inayat, my brother, was born in 1947. We called him Nannu, and Mummy naturally became so engrossed with her own child, that too a boy, that for her I slowly slipped into the background. But never with my father; I was truly his daughter.

My two passions in life were, and are, shoes and books. When he wanted to spoil me, Daddy would say, "Let's go buy some shoes." We would head up to a charming little bookshop called Happy Bookstore, which I believe still exists on Hill Road, and buy an Enid Blyton novel for a few rupees.

Because he still put me first, as one would the eldest child, I have a great relationship with my brother. At first, of course, I didn't know that he was technically my cousin, and I played with him and looked after him as any older sister would. Even after I found out, my life was so replete with love that I didn't resent him at all.

The stroke of luck that blessed Mummy with a son gave birth to a strange reputation about me. I became a living fertility charm, and childless couples would invite me to their homes in the hope of a miracle. The magic would only work, it seemed, if I stayed the night. So,

I made many visits to the homes of people who were desperate for a baby, and this became my first education in manners and socializing. These couples would be a little awkward and self-conscious around a child and it was up to me to break the ice.

I learnt to give genuine compliments, even when as young as seven or eight, about the decor or the food my host made. I would join any activity they were doing—if the lady of the house was cooking, I would follow her to the kitchen and get her talking about the dish. If there were cards on the table or I spied a collection of books or records, I would inquire about them.

Funnily enough, this reputation persisted into adulthood. In the 2000s, a couple in Navy Nagar, who had been childless for a decade, requested me to come to their home for a cup of tea. They had decided to opt for adoption after every other option, including medical, had failed and decided to try this one last thing before starting the paperwork. I warned them that my 'magic' had worked when I was a child but they were insistent. I love meeting new people, so I went over to Navy Nagar, and lo and behold, they had a baby boy within a year.

More recently, I got a call from a former student. She had come from East Africa for diction and enunciation lessons. During the course of our interactions, she confessed that she and her husband were pining for a child—they had been married for seven or eight years. She was 40 years old and felt like time was closing in on her.

"Will you pray for me?" she pleaded in a vulnerable moment. To make her feel better, I asked her to hold my hand as we said a little prayer. A year and a half later, in 2018, she rang to say she was having a baby!

Life at Villa Vazir was filled with happy camaraderie but was also a tightrope walk. After I found out I was adopted, I strived to be accepted and would always side with the majority lest they say something like, "What would you know? You were adopted." I would agree to play what they wanted to play, show fondness for the same meat. In short, I did everything to not draw attention to myself and found safety in being accepted.

It was not that I didn't have opinions; it's just that I knew what they were and it didn't diminish me in any way to keep them to myself. To this day, I don't see the point of being obnoxious and pushing my opinion in people's faces. I only give it if someone asks. If I know it's going to be unsavoury, I'll find a way of putting it palatably.

One of my earliest memories is of how we rung in Independence on August 15. We went on a family picnic to Lingmala Falls in Lonavala. Like we often would, we called for a lorry from our transport business, lined the carrier with thin, cotton mattresses, loaded up all the children, fortified ourselves with samosas and *bhajia*s and set out for a picnic. Civilization ended at Mahim Creek and though places like Sion and Chembur did exist, they were very small and were just names to us. The last outpost for our picnics or drives was Khopoli where we stopped to have an especially greasy and yellow *puri-bhaaji* before making our way up the *ghat*s on dirt roads.

The first few years after Independence, August 15 was celebrated with much gusto. All of the city would be lit up in festoons of orange, white and green blinking lights and there would be fireworks at night.

Another memory I have is of the whole family travelling to Calcutta, as it was called then, by train, for Uncle Keki and Aunty Noorjehan's wedding. Blocks of ice were placed in the middle of the train compartment to "cool" it down. This served as a makeshift air conditioning and people took turns to sit on the seats around the blocks of ice.

After the wedding, we welcomed Aunty Noorjehan with an exciting ritual. Dadima sat on a low stool with a *thaal* of gold coins and everyone was cheering and urging the veiled new bride to gather as many as she could in both palms. '*Jyada lo, jyada lo*' they chanted. All the coins that she could hold were hers to keep.

One of the tenants at Villa Vazir was PL Tandon—the head honcho at Hindustan Lever. He was married to a Swedish lady, and their daughter Maya became my first firm friend. Their home was an introduction to European sophistication and refinement. The tables were set with cutlery and serviettes to eat roasts and meatballs, so different from the Indian *thaali* system in my home. I was in awe of Maya's skills with the cutlery; she wielded the fork and knife with such ease and grace.

Mrs. Tandon maintained an elegant bathroom: in the time of bland green Hamam soaps, her wash basin would have a delicate, perfumed, shell-like hand soap. And the towels were fluffy—this was before washing machines and softeners, mind you. To this day, I have towels, tissues, soap and perfume in my powder room for guests.

Daddy was a charming businessman who knew what public relations meant before the term was coined. He owned a factory that manufactured glass vials to hold medicines, and drove around in a powder blue Dodge with pristine white seats. His best friend Naval Tata and he would often go off to Jamshedpur together to visit one Tata plant or another.

Most mornings, some acquaintance or friend would appear in Villa Vazir requesting a favour. It could be membership into a gymkhana, or assistance in smoothening official paperwork, and my father just could not say no. He would find some way to help out. To me, he seemed the most loved man in Bandra who knew everyone—from tennis coaches to politicians. He would connect people, ease situations, accompany friends to minister's offices to address grievances and find myriad ways to help a friend.

Having been taught by Europeans, Daddy was a man of polished manners and highly refined social skills and had a wide, multicultural circle of friends. He enjoyed the company of intelligent, sophisticated people, people of the world, and loved to socialize through card parties and evenings out.

Mummy was a simple lady, happy in her home and kitchen. She would spend the day in a *farack-pachedi* and only wear saris when going out for occasions such as a *majlis* (a religious and social gathering for Muslim women) or a wedding. Though Daddy taught her to speak English, she never spoke it with ease and did not enjoy my father's circle of race-goers, expats, Parsi and Anglo-

Indian businessmen, bank managers and their glamorous companions.

So, by the time I was 10, I became his social partner. I would wear a nice dress, white shoes and feel very sure of myself with my little handbag. People were amused by me and I absorbed everything I could about diplomacy and social skills.

"Everybody knows about the terrible things in life," Daddy would say about social conversations. "Let's talk about the positive things." He taught me to move from group to group at a party. "Otherwise, how will people know you are there?" he used to say. Sitting with just the people you know puts you in a comfortable rut, and by moving around you get to know new people, learn new things and grow.

It was Daddy who taught me how to hover at the edge of a chatty group, keep an ear out for a lull in the conversation and then quickly introduce oneself by saying something like, "Hi, I'm Haaji. It's so fascinating what you just said about Spain. Tell me, did you spend a lot of time there?"

He knew that to network, he needed to draw people out by getting them to talk about what they found interesting, not what he wanted to talk about. Never did he barge into a group and try to dominate it by showing off, arguing or steering the conversation.

Most importantly, he knew that true diplomacy is courtesy and kindness, it's being interested in the other person. People like and remember those who make them feel important and heard, not those who make them feel invisible and irrelevant. And Daddy knew how to do this with outmost sincerity.

Soon, people came to expect me at card parties and the races, and I enjoyed these outings. As advised by my English teacher, I honed my language skills by listening to the BBC Radio at night and also reading the newspaper. When I began accompanying my father, I realized that the news made a good and neutral conversation opener. A well-informed person has a charm of her own.

"You must bring your daughter when you come to the bank, Haaji," said Mr. Goddard, the British manager of Standard Chartered Bank. "She'll be an asset to you."

I found that though I was a child among adults, nobody dismissed me because I could speak about current affairs or at least understood the context of their conversations. I also learnt to be observant and read a room.

"Sabi, you have to become a diplomat. That is your real métier in life. You always say the right thing to the right person," Daddy would say.

The treasure I inherited from him is that he propped me up to become a whole person. I have often wondered whether I am a result of nature, i.e., Bapaji's genetics or nurture, i.e., the love and freedom my adoptive father gave me.

It's a combination of both. Had I gone back to being Abdul Hussain Thariani's daughter, I would have lived in Pakistan, never met my husband, gone to a finishing school in Switzerland or been on stage. As Haaji-bhai's daughter, I received a liberal upbringing, a convent education, the freedom to choose my life partner and exposure to many opportunities and challenges that helped me realize my genetic potential.

In the mid-1950s, as our family grew, we moved out of Villa Vazir to Sanjana Mansion in Bandra where the landlord lived on the floor below and we were amidst the East Indian and Goan Christian community. Eventually we moved to Maryville and Rickland, all within Bandra.

My father told me to observe how the Goans and the Anglo-Indians carried themselves in dresses and heels, with handbags. In our Muslim circles, the ladies only wore salwars and saris. I learnt to make *kulkul*s, marzipan sweets and jujubes, and observed the social niceties of sending Easter eggs in decorated baskets to neighbours.

The twenty-something Christian working girls became my fashion idols, particularly my neighbours Nora and Iwinka Fernandes. One of them was the top secretary at a firm. "I work five days a week and leave very early in the morning," she told me. "I keep my outfits ready for the week so that I never get up and just put anything on in a rush." They taught me to paint my nails and get manicures and pedicures. This was before beauty salons offered these services, so we friends would do it for each other. They also taught me the importance of good underwear and petticoats.

I still plan my outfits in advance for a trip, a social visit or even everyday business.

Designing the clothes was a long, detailed affair. First, the ladies of Villa Vazir or the neighbourhood would motor all the way up to Crawford Market or Colaba

Causeway once every three or four months. Even then, it was the place to go to for fabric, lace and all things beautiful. "*Mai-ji, Mai-ji,*" men with trays suspended by a belt around their necks would call out. They peddled little universes of hair clips, safety pins, and bits and bobs and we would peer over their tiny treasures.

After we bought the fabric, I would head over to Mrs. Braganza, the seamstress in our neighbourhood, for lunch. We would pore over magazines to see what Elizabeth Taylor and Audrey Hepburn were wearing, and design a similar dress for me. Christian Dior's 'New Look' was all the rage then, and within a few weeks, for a princely sum of ₹100, I would have two dresses.

Mrs. Braganza remained an integral part of my life, even after I got married and moved to South Bombay. She made my clothes until she grew too old to sew.

As I grew older, I went to St. Joseph's Convent. My parents insisted I walk there; they thought I would be spoilt with a car and driver. At St. Joseph's, we were taught by English and Irish nuns such as Sister Margaret and Sister Cecelia. An Anglo-Indian lady called Mrs. Bradley taught us English and managed to impart her love for the language to the students.

I was good at History and English, but really suffered in Maths. I was the best at being a clown and mimicking the teachers, and all of us made fun of the Maths teacher, Mr. Gangadhar. Thus, I would find myself standing in the corner of the classroom as punishment very often. But I learnt to carry a pencil and sharpener with me and would pretend to sharpen my pencil should Mother Superior pass by. "How many times do you do that?" she asked me once. "I... I like a sharp tip," I mumbled.

I wasn't very interested in sports either, though I was in the netball team; words really became my toys at this age. I would listen to the BBC Radio every night under the covers and write down words that I did not understand, for example, 'procrastination'. In school, I would ask Mrs. Bradley what they meant and how to pronounce them.

Around the time I was 10, I became enamoured by boarding schools described in the books of Enid Blyton, which I would devour. I began to beg and harangue my father to send me to one, even as he tried to tell me that it was a very hard life. "What you read and the reality are two different things," he tried to explain to me, but I would not let it go.

St. Joseph's had a residential school in Panchgani and I was transferred there. My uncle, Yaseen, had a touch of TB around the time and was renting Kashana Cottage in Panchgani. So I was able to see him over the weekends, but soon after getting into boarding school, I realized I hated it. There were no midnight feasts and the girls were quite cliquish, so I didn't really make any friends. There was a hell lot of discipline. It was not like the books at all.

But after all the fuss I had made with my father, I told myself that I better learn to like it. My escape from this prison of my own making came in a very painful way. I was playing on the seesaw one day and the other girl bumped down so hard that the handle slammed into my chin and sent my teeth flying out. My mouth was full of blood and I was sent to the infirmary while we waited for my father to motor up from Bombay the next day.

The only dentist in Panchgani was about a hundred years old, so it was a given that I would have to go to Bombay to have my teeth fixed. I saw the window of opportunity and bolted through it—I told Daddy that I wanted to come back home and I think he was relieved.

It took a long time for my gums to heal, but the doctor said I was lucky because the teeth I lost were extra ones anyway, which a dentist would have had to surgically remove to prevent crowding. As a result, I never needed braces.

Once home, I enrolled back into my old school in Bandra. I was about 12 at this point, and grew to be good at expressive recitation. It was here that I was first exposed to the magic of theatre. The Kendals came to town with their theatre company, Shakespeareana, and performed at the St. Stanislaus Auditorium. I was captivated and thought that to travel around the world and make a living being someone else on stage was the biggest adventure.

The only time my father came to school was to enrol me and after that he never saw the inside of its hallways. My mother never even saw my school. My folks didn't come to talk to the teachers to enquire about my progress, pay the fees, a royal sum of ₹14 per month, or attend PTAs like all the other parents. I was in a play once, playing a character in a castle, and my parents didn't attend that performance either. I suppose they were confident that I was independent enough to handle paying the fees all by myself and be responsible about my studies, but I did feel a little neglected and left out.

Instead of Board exams, we had the Senior Cambridge exams in those days, and after I was done, I told my father that I would like to appear for Matriculation too. He didn't understand why in the world I would want to study more. But I was nervous about passing Maths, even though I had been to tuitions to Master Menezes for a princely sum of ₹300 per month. He was an institution in himself in Bandra and would take classes for geometry and algebra. He would make all his students sit in a row and solve past papers so that we knew what to expect. I sailed through Maths because of him.

I think I caught this bug for studying and carving a career from Bapaji. He told me with great relish how he studied under a streetlight in Dongri while growing up as they were too poor to afford oil for lamps. All my sisters and cousins just finished school and got married, but I had got into my head to go to outer space.

This was also the time that USA and USSR were locked in a space race and the newspapers were talking about the Soviet Union's Sputnik 1, Earth's first artificial satellite. I was determined to become a cosmonaut, and thought I would have to go to the USSR to do this. It was the excitement of the unknown that drove me. All the other professions seemed so dry! To become a doctor would be to be like Dr. Leander, the physician at Villa Vazir—a squat man who drove a black Morris Minor and was always in good 'spirits'.

So, I set out to study for the Matriculation. A girl

called Batool, the daughter of the Nawab of Cambay, was also to appear for the same exams and her mother requested that she come study with me. She had many marriage proposals waiting but could not accept any of them unless she passed out of school. Her mother felt that I would be a good influence on her.

Batool would come over in her long limousine and we would start studying at around 4 am fuelled by a flask of tea Mummy kept on the desk. It was a whole new syllabus so I would just mug things up. I coiled myself into such a frenzy over these exams that my hair literally came out in chunks and my father got me a tonic called Koko from the chemist to stop this.

The crucial difference between Daddy and Bapaji came to the fore during my visits to Pakistan every year. Where Daddy thought life's manuals were *How to Win Friends and Influence People* and *How to Stop Worrying and Start Living*, Bapaji held the *Quran* above all else.

I must have been around six when I started to take a Constellation flight to Pakistan every year to spend months with my biological family. Home life in Karachi was startlingly different. We lived in a villa designed by my father in the heart of the city.

Fazl-O-Rabbi was an open house with a dining room at the heart of it. A samovar of tea would be lit every morning with small cups encircling it. This was the signal that anybody, across classes, was welcome in this home. Any time one would pass through the room, it was the done thing to pour yourself a cup before moving on. To me, it seemed that the whole house—its inhabitants and visitors—were powered by this sweet, milky tea.

Jinnah had kept his word to my father and made him part of many developmental projects in the freshly-minted country. Innumerable people would pass through Fazl-O-Rabbi every day because my father was so well-connected. It was a common thing to go meet Abdul Hussain bhai, as he was called, when one came to Karachi.

Despite this success in two nations, Bapaji had not forgotten his roots. Once a week, children from an orphanage—a new one each time—would be invited home for a meal, and we would serve them food and eat with them.

Another story he loved to tell was about how he met his close friend and associate, Uncle Bunkle. Bapaji was headed to Sir JJ School of Arts and Architecture to give the entrance exams for the architecture course. Riding in the tram, he was worried about how he would draw without the required geometry instruments. Just then, he spied a boy admiring his shiny, new, foreign-bought compass box. "Are you going to appear for the exams at JJ too?" Bapaji asked. The young man nodded. "May I borrow your instruments when you are done?" The boy agreed.

The examinees had to draw the Taj Mahal, an elephant and a palm tree. Bapaji decided to be clever about it: he drew the palm tree in the foreground, since it was the easiest to draw, then the Taj Mahal at mid-distance, but smaller to seem like it was far away, and so that he didn't have to draw the details. And the elephant, even smaller.

Both of them passed the exams and Bunkle and Bapaji became firm friends, and later, associates. When he was leaving the country, Bapaji presented a bungalow in

Bandra to Uncle Bunkle as a token of his gratitude and friendship, and the family lives in it till today.

My father was also famous for his unbending integrity; there was not a touch of corruption in him. When he retired, Pakistan's architectural body honoured him with a necklace of gold guineas as recognition of his honesty.

Bapaji was also very social but in a different way. He would mix only with Muslims, and go to *mushaira*s, poetry recitals and religious meetings. His throne was the four-seater sofa swing on the patio, with a fountain in the background. All around were low seating arrangements with bolsters and pillows. If ever he caught hold of me when he was in a reflective and talkative mood on this *jhula*, I knew I would be stuck there until someone relieved me.

But I loved listening to my father discuss the largeness of life and our purpose in it, which Daddy never talked to me about. Though my exposure to Bapaji was brief, it was intense and I treasure it.

He would take such pains to reveal the beauty of the *Quran* to me, reciting the *surah*s, appealing to my poetic nature and love for imagery. Once when I was nine or ten, he called out to me from his throne. "What are the things you are surest of in life?" he asked. "I'm sure I am going to the bazaar today with Baima," I replied, referring to my biological mother. "We're going in a rickshaw to *sadar* (the market) to buy a nice outfit..."

"But what if Baima falls sick?" he asked.

"Well, then we won't go to the bazaar..." I replied.

"What else are you sure about?"

"I'm sure I am going to grow up to be a good girl..."

"What if there is an accident and you are stuck in bed and can't grow up?"

"Well yes... I am not sure of growing up either."

"So, what are you really sure of?"

"Well, then I can be sure of nothing. If I say 'the day will end,' you'll find something negative to say about that too..." I whined.

"No," he said patiently, "I'm telling you something very positive: the only thing you can be sure about is death. And that is the eventuality we are least prepared for."

"What do you mean 'least prepared'?"

"What are you doing to go towards that big moment when you meet your maker? You are just ambling from day to day. You have to do all the good things in life, be charitable towards the poor to be close to God. So that when you go, he is there to receive you with open arms."

This stuck with me: the certainty that God watches over us and that we have to answer to him.

I used to think that he had this urgency to impart *sikhaman* (teachings, in Urdu) because our time together was so short, but now I know it was because I was receptive to it.

Funnily, neither of my mothers talked to me about life or the world. Our conversations would be about what I wanted for dinner or clothes.

Baima's passion was flowers. Not only did she personally tend to and nurture a beautiful rose garden, she also mainly wore floral prints and embroidered flowers on to her shopping bags—cloth bags with wooden handles. People from all over would come to see the roses and the landscaping of her gardens.

Her pet topic to chat about was the wealth of her hair before motherhood. She was a small woman and her hair was so long that they had to construct a special stool which she would climb up on so that it just touched the floor and didn't trail on it. The servants then would fan out her hair (she could only wash it on sunny days because there were no hairdryers in those days) to dry it.

Bapaji and Baima's marriage started on a very curious note. My mother was a true innocent and was married to my father when she was 14. She didn't know that there has to be a physical relationship between a husband and a wife. She thought you just get married and Allah gives you children. She was scandalized when my father told her about the birds and the bees and wanted nothing to do with it. She wouldn't allow him near her and it took months to sink in that sexual relations were natural within a marriage.

Theirs grew into a strong, enviable bond thereafter. Both of them were poets and there was an Elizabeth Barrett–Robert Browning element to their relationship.

She took charge of their financial planning as Bapaji had no idea about money matters. He didn't even know how much to charge for his services and could not be bothered to learn about how to manage or invest his earnings. He was an artist and visionary, dabbling in poetry and water colours. "Architecture is the mother of all arts," he would say. Whatever money he made, he would come and deposit it with my mother, who would then invest it.

She was very much like her mother, our Dadima of Villa Vazir. She had everything at her fingertips—she knew how much money was in which bank and which building to buy as an investment. She invested most of the money in real estate and gold in such a way that all of us got an equal inheritance.

Every day, Baima would give Bapaji five rupees for his day's expenses and his needs were so few that often the money would remain unspent in his pocket.

When Bapaji was on his deathbed, he urged my brothers to take care of Baima because he knew she would not live long without him. He was the centre of her existence. And sure enough, nine months after his departure, while she was tending to her beloved roses, Baima just sank to the ground and breathed her last.

My siblings led a regimented, insular existence. Though they had the means, they did not travel abroad or even within the country. Bapaji was a strict but involved father and directed the lives of all his children. He knew the strengths and aptitudes of each son and daughter. He set up a business for the brother who could not apply himself to studies and pushed Saleem, my eldest brother, to become an architect and an engineer because he knew his strengths.

Yet, their opportunities to explore the world outside their country and religion were limited.

Aghast at my lack of religious education, Bapaji felt he had failed in his duty as a father, and it was something he would have to answer for when he met his maker. "I will go up there and I will be examined by God. Why did I give my blood away? 'Couldn't you take care of her that you gave her away? Now she is not informed about Islam...'" he would say. "You should fast, you should pray, you should not show too much skin," he would tell this Bandra girl who wore only frocks and sleeveless dresses to socials at Bandra Gymkhana. It was like asking me to join a convent! My sisters began lending me their pajamas which I would wear under my dresses even at home.

So, he took it upon himself to teach me about Islam, but he did it adroitly because he knew he could not bully me into following it by incessant lecturing.

He was gentle in his instruction. Seeing my siblings keep the *roza* during Ramazan, I wanted to join in too. I must have been six or seven and Bapaji knew I was too little to undergo strict fasting. "Why don't you keep two half *roza*s," he said. "Just don't eat anything till lunch. And then we'll stitch them into a full one."

The only outings in Pakistan were those with a religious motive. Either it was a *Gham ka Majlis*, which means a sad one when the Prophet was martyred, or it would be *Khushi ka Majlis* on auspicious days. We never went out with the sole purpose of having a meal outside or even drink a cup of tea at someone else's house.

These visits gave me a chance to bond with my siblings. My sister Mumtaz was very confident and had a beautiful voice; I was a great admirer of her public skills. She used to be called to sing at *majlis*es; that was the only time it was acceptable for a woman to sing in public. Sing the wrong kind of song, say one from a film or in English, and you were out of the marriage scene as someone too bold.

I too volunteered to sing at my brother Saleem's wedding. Everybody expected me to sing a religious hymn, but I only knew the songs we learnt in school and sang 'Wonderful Copenhagen' in front of 200 people. There was pin-drop silence and everyone was aghast. But I was so pleased with myself! I turned around to see my brother shaking.

Mumtaz fell in love with a good-looking man called Afzal who came from an Irani family. Iranis then were considered a little too liberal. I would be their cover-up when they met, and when my father found out, he flipped.

Marriage, according to him, had to be arranged through the right channels. It had to go through our mother and it would have to be from our Khoja community and even the same *chotti jamat*—Ishna Shari. But my sister held her ground and married Afzal.

When the time came, Bapaji didn't approve of my match with Chotu, nor did my birth parents approve of me going to Switzerland—they found it all too liberal. But Daddy stood his ground and said that this is what Sabi wants and she wouldn't be happy with anybody else.

I also realized what jealousy is when I visited Pakistan. While my older sister Mumtaz loved me very much, Shabnam, who was born immediately after me, would resent my visits because everyone would make such a fuss. Every now and then, she would bite me or pinch me.

I was so worried that I once wrote to Mumtaz, saying,

'Dear Mumhtaaz (sic),

I cannot come to Krachi as Shabnam bits me (sic). Please tell her not to bit (sic) me please.'

This is also where I met my first and only boyfriend. He was the neighbour's son and we would chat across the garden wall. I must have been 13 or 14 and Ghulam Abbas was tall and good looking, and a reserve for the Pakistan cricket team. We became pen pals and it was a budding romance. Of course, Chotu came a few years later and blitzed everything.

Had I lived in Pakistan in that house, surely something would have come out of it because our fathers were very good friends and Gullu came from the same background and community.

I never really told anyone about him, except for Chotu, of course. Then, in 2015, this Israeli mind reader came to town and of all the people in the audience, called me up on stage, and of all things, asked me if I remembered the name of my first boyfriend.

Then, he asked me to turn my back on the audience and actively think about his name while he wrote it down on a piece of paper. Nobody in the whole of Bombay knew about Ghulam, but sure enough, he had written Gullu on the paper!

If you ask me whether I am like my Bapaji or Daddy, I would say I am a product of both. I would like to think I have Bapaji's integrity, propensity for hard work and the hunger to study, but I am Haaji's liberal, practical daughter who does not live within the boundaries of caste, religion or language.

And there is no greater proof of this than the fact that all my children married partners of different religions and my grandchildren are of different religions.

2

The European Adventure

IN 1957, AN INTRODUCTION to Ahmed Hussein Merchant opened up the world to me. Till then, I was a girl from Bandra who had eaten in a restaurant perhaps once, and that too at Mc Ronall's mom-and-pop bakery-eatery where we had chicken puffs and cream rolls. In 1958, I had to board a plane, travel through Europe, admit myself into a finishing school in Switzerland and live on my own for a year. Looking back, I don't know how I did it at a time when I was not even 16!

By the time I was 14 and finishing school, marriage proposals had begun trickling in. One of them was from the illustrious Merchant family of Bhavnagar that lived in South Bombay.

Shirin Banu had seen me at *majlis*es in Bombay and liked my open, friendly and adaptable manners. She hoped to secure me as a wife for one of her sons and sent a go-between to my grandmother.

I didn't like the idea of meeting a prospective groom at all. "Am I a goat or a cow to be paraded in front of a potential buyer?" I asked my father churlishly. I was still holding on to the dream of going to Russia to be a cosmonaut. “Let’s take it one step at a time,” Daddy said, “Why don’t we discuss this proposal right now and if you don’t like it, we’ll see what you want to do in life.”

So, one day, Fatima and Banu-ma, Chotu’s eldest sisters, dropped into our home in Bandra. I was sitting barefoot at the dining table, doing my homework. I thought they were visiting my mother but did think it a bit odd as we never had any visitors, apart from Bapaji and Baima or other relatives.

The sisters urged me to join them in the living room and we chatted about this and that, mostly what I was studying in school.

I didn’t think about it much and got on with life—clearing my Cambridge exams, finishing school and taking on Matriculation.

Soon after, Uncle Yaseen drove me up to Bombay Gymkhana to meet Ahmed, or Chotu as he liked to be called, and discreetly excused himself. My mother—her wardrobe full of pale nylon and georgette saris—insisted I buy special silk for the occasion. It was a bright yellow *kanjeevaram* sari with an orange border, which in retrospect, was hideous!

I remember the meeting vividly, and not only because it was my first ‘date’. In hindsight, it seems so awkward to meet a stranger with the intention of gauging whether we would be able to spend a lifetime together. And that too as a teenager, because I must have been just short of 16 then.

To be perfectly frank, I fell for Chotu’s looks. At 22, he was a natty dresser, and on that day at the Bombay

Gymkhana, he was wearing a blue striped shirt and grey trousers. He had striking light blue, earnest eyes and seemed like a good human being, which was appealing.

We walked the length of the Gymkhana's veranda while chatting about our hopes and families. He asked me what I liked, and I talked about Shakespeare, the arts and theatre, my dream to become a cosmonaut—things he was not interested in at all. He told me about his work and business.

He later told me that he liked that I had cultivated a mind of my own. The thing that made him sit up and notice me was how easily I expressed myself. He asked why I was wearing a sari, and I replied that I hated them but my mother had insisted I do. It was uncommon in those days for girls to disagree with someone or voice an opinion.

We ended the meeting wanting to see more of each other, and our families were thrilled.

My future now firmly set in India and not outer space, I enrolled in Nirmala Niketan at Churchgate to study Home Science. Chotu's youngest sister—Zubi, short for Zubeida—was my classmate there, as was Veena Thacker, his future sister-in-law.

We were all in awe of Zubi and the family's international exposure. She would sashay into college with a darling little leather handbag bought from a jaunt to Italy or England, while the rest of us went to Colaba and Crawford Market to buy fashion maybe once a year.

This was in the days before the opening up of the economy of the country. Imported things were elusive and exclusive, and to be able to buy them on a trip abroad was even rarer. Not too many people went overseas, certainly not with the casual ease of the Merchants. It was a privilege enjoyed only by those in power or Anglo-Indians.

Even readymade garments hadn't dawned on the horizon yet—all our clothes were stitched either at home by mothers or seamstresses. The only 'readymade' garments one could buy were socks and undergarments from Rajsi Bros on Colaba Causeway. There were T-shirts, for sure, but meant for sports and were not considered casual wear yet.

Veena was a model and we were all a little envious of her lithe figure. The regulation those days was a cotton or synthetic sari from Khatau or Calico mills, worn with cute Magyar-sleeved blouses that dropped over our shoulders (only the very daring wore sleeveless!). We nicknamed her 'half-yard' after her audacious strappy blouses that required half the span of cloth of regular sari blouses.

Chotu and I continued seeing each other. I found that like me, he was an extrovert and very open to new experiences. He enjoyed the fine things in life, most unique among them being shopping! And unlike other men, he was so secure that he had no qualms admitting when he didn't know something.

On our first dinner at the Greens Hotel at the Taj, he asked me what I would like to eat. "Crabs and lobsters," I replied. "Oh, I don't know what that is but I would like to give it a try," he said. So, we ordered the Lobster Thermidor and I showed him how to eat it! It really struck me that he was confident enough around a woman to admit when he didn't know something, even if on a date.

I knew things were getting serious when Chotu popped around at my home on my birthday. I was sitting about in a purple sari and chappals and he asked my mother's whether he could take me to his home. She agreed, and we left without me making any special effort to polish myself up for the first formal meeting with the prospective in-laws.

He hadn't had the foresight to buy me a present beforehand and scampered about at the last minute. Zubi helped him out by giving her silver-backed hairbrush set, which he hurriedly got polished and presented to me. And then, in all innocence, told me where he got it!

While we were riding up the elevator to their apartment, Chotu playfully took off my glasses. "You put those right back," I said. "But you look prettier without them," he said. "I want to meet them exactly as I am—glasses and all," I said. He gave up with a laugh.

His family was thrilled to have me and we all went out to Volga's for dinner. Chotu's father was so particular that when he realized there would be 13 people at the table which was considered unlucky, he had Chotu's niece Yasmin woken up to join us. I remained observant through the dinner and spoke to everyone at the table, even the young ones. As a special treat, they ordered an exquisite Baked Alaska for me, which is an ice cream with a meringue shell that is quickly baked and presented before the ice cream melts.

I soon told my father I would like to get engaged, much to his chagrin.

"What? Are you going to marry the first thing in pants I introduce you to?" he said alarmed. He was quite insistent that I meet other boys, but I saw no point of shopping around when I had made up my mind.

Now my family began dissuading me! "You had better be careful," said Dadima. "It won't be easy pleasing all eight people in the family."

The other thing Dadima warned me about was the family's love of a game of chance, which had driven Chotu's grandfather—who owned a small oil mill in Bhavnagar—to bankruptcy. The business community remembered him coming to the bazaar with his *topi* worn the other way around—a public communication of the crisis. "It's in their blood, you are not going to escape it," warned Dadima. "They do what they like." I was confused; she had introduced me to this boy and now she was trying to dissuade me from marrying him.

As always, I made optimism my choice and threw caution to the wind. "Am I going to look at everything that's negative?" I thought to myself, "I'm a happy person; I'm diplomatic. I can turn things around and be a positive influence."

Dadima imparted another canny piece of advice. When she sensed things were getting serious between Chotu and myself, she called me into her room: "Listen, they are going to ask you to choose from a spread of diamonds. Don't pick the largest stone, you'll seem greedy; and don't pick the smallest one, it will say like you have no self-worth. Pick something in the middle; that's the size that will suit you anyway."

We got engaged at the Merchant family home in Marine Drive around close family members and then had lunch. Chotu gave me a ring with the diamond I had chosen, surrounded by baguettes. My father went out on a limb and got him a diamond too. Uniquely, our families did not discuss horoscopes or assets to decide whether we were a good match—it was based purely on compatibility.

We were set to get married about six months later, but cancer claimed my father-in-law and as per tradition, the nuptials had to be postponed for a year.

My father was not happy with a long engagement. "You can't keep up this pace; you'll have to slow down completely," said Daddy. "Suppose this goes on for a year and you both decide not to get married?"

By now, Chotu and I were seeing each other every day. He had become great friends with my father and would come over after work. We would then go for a drive around Bandra, have an ice cream, or sit on a bench at Carter Road and talk about our day. My father's fears were completely unfounded because my strict 'Christian' school values would not let me venture beyond holding hands.

When Daddy told Chotu about his reservations, my fiancé suggested I go to a finishing school in Switzerland. "She'll be exposed to another way of life," he reasoned.

"Look," said Daddy, "I am a simple man of mediocre means. I can take care of my family, but I can't afford to send my daughter to Switzerland."

Chotu gallantly offered to use his inheritance to

sponsor my education—no strings attached. Daddy accepted this, but Dadima was not too pleased.

"It's such a long break," she said. "When you come back, they'll say you were tainted by the West and nobody will want to marry you."

I spent a few turbulent days not understanding why my fiancé wanted to send me away. "It's very important that you have a choice," he said. "A period of separation will be good. You are too young and have not been exposed to the world outside Bandra. You've never even left India! I'm the first boy you've met. Suppose you meet someone else you think you might love?"

I didn't agree at all and certainly did not want to audition suitors for a whole year in Switzerland. In retrospect, I realize how generous, wise and confident he was even in his early 20s.

I was to travel with Mary Milford, Chotu's American sister-in-law. She had met his brother Mammu while she was studying at Wellesley and was about five or six years older than me. She was a woman of the world, having attended university, and lived alone and knew how to be stylishly turned out. A wholesome all-American girl, she had a fondness for short, trapeze dresses and T-bar sandals.

She wisely took me shopping before the trip so that we could buy some grown-up things, like a pair each of black-and-beige, low-heeled, almond-toed shoes to replace my school girlish Mary Janes.

Travel, in those days, was an adventure but the process was much simpler. One would check in the luggage at the counter, and there was no security check. The Customs officials inspected your handbag, took a look at your ticket and then you walked out of the door and towards the waiting aircraft.

Of all the things I could wear on a flight, I chose a sari! I must have been out of my ever-loving mind, but I felt I had to make the effort because so many people were coming to see me off. Most of my family was there and they garlanded me and pushed packets of sweets and dry fruits into my arms. In my handbag, I carried all the cash I needed for my school fees and traveller's cheques from American Express for other expenses. On my lap was a file with the flight tickets, train tickets, and all the documents for my admission into La Chatelaine Institut des Jeunes Filles in Saint-Blaise, Switzerland.

Instead of going directly to Switzerland, Mary and I were to wander around the continent for a couple of weeks. Chotu had instructed her to make the most of our trip and show me all the sights and sounds.

And it truly was an awakening.

We first landed in Beirut, Lebanon just as winter was approaching. Each man and woman who passed by was more sophisticated than the one before them. All the ladies wore beautiful scarves, elegant shoes and hats, and trailed perfume. I was so glad that Mary had taken me shopping before we left India, but I still felt inadequate in the Paris of the East.

The sensory treat was not restricted to only the eyes. Never shy of trying out new flavours, I tasted grilled fish with a lemon sauce, olives and hummus, and all kinds of Lebanese bread.

Beirut was also where I went to a discotheque for the first time. Mary nursed her wine and I my Coke as I watched girls in miniskirts dance with slick boys. Dancing was still primarily a courting ritual—you went to the dance floor if a boy asked you. Gangs of friends of the same, or even mixed gender did not occupy the floor. As I took it all in, wide-eyed, a young man asked me to dance. "I wouldn't, if I were you," said Mary, and I demurred.

Next came Italy, and Mary took me to a salon to get my hair done. I didn't even know you could have someone else wash your hair in a basin and style it! European hairdressing was a luxurious experience. We were plied with wine and coffee while we waited in a hushed salon, the tables heaved with fashion magazines. Once in the chair, the chatty Italian hairdresser was effusive with compliments and adroitly piled my shoulder-length tresses into a bouffant, the style of the day.

As we stepped out, a man riding a Lambretta spun around and exclaimed, "La Bella!" He happened to have a camera slung around his neck and charmingly asked for a photograph.

How different this was from visiting Madame in Bandra to get my hair cut, which is surely how things must be done in prison! 'Madame' as she insisted on being called, was one of those Anglo-Indians or English people who didn't go back after Independence. She ran a 'parlour' out of a room in her house. You would call for an appointment, or make a visit, and be the only one there. There was a lone chair in front of the mirror and one beehive hairdryer in the corner, which I hadn't had the honour of using. No posters on the wall, no magazines and no chit-chat. Madame made no conversation, not even about what kind of cut you would like. She would silently assess your hair, decide what she wanted to do with it, cut it dry and send you off without a styling tip or a 'see you soon'!

We explored Rome as we did Beirut, going on guided tours in the morning and exploring the nightlife after sunset. One evening, I decided to go into the city alone and found myself in a fancy restaurant atop a hill overlooking the city. I ordered a meal of fish (that is still the meat I am most comfortable with since I had it for breakfast through my childhood) and an exquisite dessert made of sliced oranges and burnt peel arranged around the plate. I sat there satiated and enchanted with this new turn in life. When the bill came, I was horrified by the expense of it all! Luckily, I had a 20-dollar bill—which was quite a lot in those days—tucked into the back of my bag.

We landed in London next and everything I had read about came alive—red double-decker buses, Trafalgar Square, Buckingham Palace, Westminster Abbey, the House of Parliament that I saw on the label of HP sauce while growing up...

Mary took me to Simpsons on the Strand where we had delicious roast beef and Yorkshire pudding. Then came guided tours of the Tower of London, and evenings were spent taking in musical shows. Professor Higgins's mezzanine library in *My Fair Lady* made such an impression on me that I vowed to have one of my own. Mary and I also went to the exclusive Wig and

Pen club near Fleet Street, where lawyers and journalists exchanged news. Finally, leaving Mary in London, I arrived in Geneva alone and took a train to a little village close by called Saint-Blaise.

When I went to see the principal, Monsieur Jobin, to pay my fees, he asked if I spoke any French. I informed him I didn't. "Oh, we only speak in French here..." he said. "Well, then I'll learn," I said determinately.

So, just as I had polished my English diction and pronunciation by listening to the radio, I set out to learn this new language from scratch. I signed up for French classes, armed myself with a little handbook of French phrases and went about translating as I spoke to my fellow students.

The school was on top of a hill. At the bottom was a village dotted with little cottages, some of which hosted the students. I lived in a cottage with about six bedrooms on the upper floor. There were two girls to each room and I shared mine with Shirley Mataxis who was American. She was the only one I spoke to in English, and that too in the privacy of our room. We ate our meals in school, but I always stopped for a flaky cornet filled with fresh cream at the neighbourhood patisserie before climbing uphill.

In the cottage, Madame imposed a 7 pm curfew, which all the girls tossed aside. They would climb down the window using bedsheets to meet various suitors while I stayed back to work on my French. "Just because you are engaged you don't have to be a nun," my friends would tease me. "Well, I'm not being a nun," I would say. "I've given my word." "Well, don't tell anyone we've gone," they would say as they slipped out the window, leaving me alone with my French books.

Of course, I was surrounded by temptation and my friends were aghast that I was already engaged to be married. I had an enlarged photograph of Chotu, taken on a trip to Mahabaleshwar with his Rolleiflex, in which he sat languidly in a rowboat on the lake. It was pinned on a board by my bed. Shirley would cheekily wish him good night at bedtime. Truth is, I was still a dutiful girl who offered namaz once a day, and abstained from pork and alcohol (though I certainly made up for that in my later years).

The finishing school really excelled at making us accomplished and polished human beings. It was a time for exploring ourselves, finding out who we were and how to play the best game with the cards we had been dealt.

The teaching staff conducted detailed interviews about what I liked so they could suggest classes. I wasn't interested in sports but loved horses because of my father's fondness for races, so I took up dressage. A talent for charcoals led me to a sketching class at the University of Neuchâtel for nudes and still life where a paid model would come and undress for us. I was scandalized at first, but soon grew used to it.

We learnt to make our own clothes, which gave me an understanding of my body, helped develop my style and taught me to adapt fashion to my taste. I learnt early on that large prints would overwhelm my slight frame and began to lean towards elegant fabrics in pastel shades.

I took a class in psychology and learnt about French cuisine, how to plan dinners and run a beautiful home. Once a week, a voice and diction teacher taught us enunciation.

Away from the classrooms, a deeper education came from my schoolmates. All the girls would sit together in classes and during breaks with others from their own countries—the Germans with the Germans, and so on. As the lone Indian, and my father's daughter, I flitted from gang to gang, picking up phrases from their native languages, and observing their body language and manner of speaking. With the Americans, I could speak freely, while with the British, I learnt to be more reserved and down-to-earth.

Most of the girls came from Europe's finest families and went home for holidays and long weekends. They knew I couldn't do the same and extended warm invitations for me to come and live with them.

I would save up my pocket money and stay with a different friend each time, absorbing Europe not as a tourist but from a natural home environment.

Shirley's father, an American General, was posted at Wiesbaden in Germany and I spent a week with them and learnt the meaning of Thanksgiving. Theirs was a relaxed American household and we would head out for burgers or to the P-Ex to buy American home essentials such as processed cheese and cans of baked beans.

Paulo—short for Paule-France Elvinger—invited me to her family chateau in Évecquemont. They owned Philips and all the women wore Dior while I wore my little frocks and skirt-sets made by Mrs. Braganza. Her sister was coming out at the debutante ball that year, and a coiffeuse from Alexandre de Paris came to do her hair. She wore a delicate white gossamer gown from Dior, of course, and we all sat around as the fitters put the finishing touches on it. Her hair was bedecked with small silver combs encrusted with diamonds. From the Elvinger women, I learnt to never go out in public without putting on lipstick and doing my hair.

Valeria Ramaciotti taught me about *la dolce vita* the way only Italians can, and the importance of a good handbag. During the few days that we spent with her family in Milan, she threw away my Bombay satchel and made me get a chic black 'borsa' with a grosgrain handle and a little bow—just big enough to hold a compact, lipstick and a kerchief. She taught me to use garter belts and how to carefully file my nails and roll stockings up and down so as not to ladder them.

Valeria and her mother would do daughter–mother brunches, drinks and dinners—rituals I hadn't seen in India.

"It's too gauche to order the bill immediately after a meal," she told me once. "You have to order an espresso and enjoy it slowly. Then casually gesture for the cheque." And so, I learnt to linger over meals as the ladies drew out elegant ebony holders for their sophisticated slim cigarettes.

All the things I absorbed during my stay in Europe manifested in my life through the years. I developed a taste for Continental living—of camembert and blue cheese for dessert, cold cuts and salad for quick lunches, formality at mealtimes, even at home; and an atmosphere of elegance and chivalry. Scarves and brooches have become my trademark. Even today, when I see a new way of wearing a scarf, I ask the person to show me how to do it.

Most importantly, I learnt the maxim that has served me all my life. It came back to me on stage in the form of my parting line as Blanche DuBois in *A Streetcar Named Desire*: Always rely on the kindness of strangers.

I needed so much guidance that year and was so often among strangers with whom I didn't share a language. But I learnt that people like to be asked for help. The key is to look around for someone approachable—not a person engrossed in doing something—and interject politely.

All my 'nun-ish' behaviour paid off at the end of the year when our French teacher, Madame Perrin, who was considered quite a fearsome monster, told the whole class to stand up and applaud me as she presented me with a certificate—I could now converse fluently in French.

Soon, it was time for me to make my way back to India, but not before I shopped for our new marital home—dinnerware, glassware and a radiogram. I asked my friends and teachers for the best place to buy these, and everyone unanimously directed me to Rosenthal's in Geneva. I chose a pure ivory dinner plate with a sheaf of wheat picked out in silver, and a set of cutlery with very clean, modern lines. Our water glasses and wine glasses matched—just one deeply-engraved line swirled lazily to the top.

Chotu also asked me to buy a "heavy duty" radiogram. He meant a top-of-the-line model, but I wondered why he would ask me to pick one that would elicit a heavy customs duty! I bought a four-feet-tall polished Grundig wooden unit with a record player and a radio—the latest technology of those times.

Since all of this could not be transported by air, I had to make my way back to India by boat. Nowadays, booking any ticket is as easy as typing out this sentence, but in 1959, I had to first ask around whether there was a liner to Bombay, and then find out how to get on it!

Saint-Blaise was a little village with one store that met the villagers' basic needs, a post office, a single phone booth and a patisserie. For anything more, we had to go to Neuchâtel.

Most of us would make a trip to the neighbouring town every Saturday to buy bits and bobs, or just walk about enjoying the weather. I had a special weekly ritual—a double meringue topped with whipped cream and a lemon tea at a tea room. If I wanted to treat myself, I would have lunch at Cafe De Paris, which is now Le Relais de l'Entrecôte. It's a famous steakhouse, and I would call in advance to book a place. There was no menu as they only served one thing—thinly-sliced grilled beef steak with a complex butter and herb sauce, thinly-sliced *pomme frites* (french fries) and a salad that was a mix of lettuce and walnuts, with a delicious dressing. The waiter would come around to ask how you would want your steak and write down the preference on the sheet of paper that served as a tablecloth. With true European finesse, they wouldn't serve you all the meat at once—they would plate a few slices and keep the others warm in the kitchen. The waiters would be discreet but vigilant, and when they saw only a couple of slices left on the plate, they would bring out the rest of your meal.

When we got a chance to go to Neuchâtel together, I took Chotu straight to Cafe de Paris to eat the steak, followed by a *meringue de chiffon*, which he loved. The waiter recognized me, and I introduced him to 'my young man' whom I had missed so much.

Le Relais de l'Entrecôte now has branches across the world, and I never miss a chance to eat there. If I am in New York City for two weeks, I'll eat there at least three times.

On one of these weekend trips to Neuchâtel, I sought out a travel agent and found out about the Lloyd Triestino that sailed to Bombay, but from Naples. I booked a place on the liner, and instructed Rosenthal and Grundig to send my purchases directly to the docks in the southern Italian city. Then I made my way to Naples, which was a daunting journey.

For the first time in my life there was no one to see me off, no one to receive me and no one to accompany me on a trip. I may have landed in Europe as a naive girl from Bandra, but I had to make my way out of it as a woman of the world. I had told Chotu I would be taking the train, but he didn't seem worried. My girlfriends in school though were aghast as to how I would go alone. My three cases and I started at the train station in Neuchâtel, where I went straight to the station master's cabin. He summoned a porter to carry my cases on board and settled me down in the coupe I shared with a seedy gentleman.

Whether my precious cargo would board the liner with me weighed on my mind, but not as much as the fact that for the first time in my life no one knew where I was for very many hours. I could just disappear somewhere on the continent and no one would know where to find me. If there was any trouble, I would have to alight at the nearest station in an alien country, my three cases in tow, and the people I could call for help, after I had located a phone booth, would be my school. There was just no way I could call my father or Chotu all the way in India, not that they would even be able to help me.

It surprised me that my parents and Chotu were so nonchalant and so confident of my abilities that they didn't even blink at the thought of what seemed a perilous journey to me. Today, in the age of cell phones and texts, we are able to keep in touch with our loved ones every step of the way. But back then, it was like travelling through a dark tunnel and I could breathe easy only once I alighted safely in Naples.

I had only a few hours in the city before I embarked on the last leg of my journey home.

Onboard the liner Lloyd Triestino, I met the flamboyant Laila Talukdar, who steered my style in a different direction. Laila, who was in her prime by then, was a well-known lady of Calcutta society and of Persian descent. I hadn't anticipated the social life onboard a liner where people played cards or Mahjong during the day and dressed for dinner.

My suitcase held demure pastel and khaki tweed suits, mostly stitched by myself in school, the odd summer dress and one black-and-gold sari. "You should wear bright colours!" Laila would instruct. "Pull your hair up. You have a great bust line; show off your collarbones."

In the time we spent with each other, Laila showed me how to pile my hair up in a knot to accentuate my neck, and sparked a love for statement jewellery. She made me bring out my sari and wear it to dinner one evening and lent me a chunky layered necklace.

Laila was a master of dramatic entrances. At the Captain's Ball, she wore a shocking pink silk sari and instead of a blouse, just wound the *pallu* tightly around her bust and threw the rest of it over her shoulder. As she descended the grand staircase, she stopped at the landing for effect and pulled on her long cigarette holder. "Laila! You can make out the shape of everything!" I said, scandalized. "Well, darling," she replied calmly, "that's the point." When I bumped into Laila 10–15 years later, the only thing that had changed about her was that she was wearing a blouse!

After about 10 days, when the ship finally docked at Bombay, the smell of the tropical harbour was the first thing that hit me. It struck me how hot, heavy and humid my city was, more so because I was wearing a self-stitched lime green tweed skirt suit! But as I walked down the gangway, amidst all the chaos of the docks and the flurry of porters, I saw my fiancé.

"Well, do you still want to marry me?" Chotu asked.

3

The Child Bride

ON FEBRUARY 25, 1960, about five months after I returned from Switzerland (and after I reassured Chotu that my ardour for him had not diminished), we got married.

Plunged back into humid, coastal weather after a year in the pristine Alps, I fell ill in the weeks following my return from Switzerland. I lost all the weight I put on courtesy the cream cornets and double meringues, and had just about recovered on my wedding day.

Till this day I don't know how Daddy pieced together the money for the wedding and the trousseau. We were still living on rent in Bandra and Daddy ran a small business. The Merchants, gracious about the gap in our financial realities, adjusted to our scale of celebration. This mutual respect became the foundation of our marriage.

Still, Daddy must have had to stretch himself or dip into his savings to buy me a diamond wedding set and a diamond ring for Chotu. We drove right up to Tribhovandas Bhimji Zaveri in Zaveri Bazaar—hard to imagine today—and I chose a minimalist classic collar of small diamonds with a row of emerald dots under it. It was paired with gold hoops and a matching bracelet.

The trousseau comprised just three saris: a white georgette one from Charni Road for the *nikah*, a maroon silk drape with dark grey embroidery for the *satara* ceremony after the wedding, and a chamois silk ecru one for the reception.

That sari was my big indulgence. The Merchant sisters told me about the Italian lady, Virginia Malhotra, who lived on Peddar Road. She did the clothes for all the ladies of high society. The Italian silk came from a friendly neighbourhood smuggler and Virginia advised stripes in a dull silver thread running diagonally to give me height. I carried an envelope clutch made from the same fabric, and Chinese cobblers—who sat behind the Taj Mahal hotel in Colaba—made me matching white satin heels. I wore art deco jewellery from the Merchant family jeweller, Hirabhai, and topped everything off with a delicate tiara bought in Switzerland.

The *nikah* was held at my home, Ritland, on Bandra's Carter Road where Chotu was shown my face in a mirror. We affirmed, in front of witnesses, that we agreed to the match and signed the contract.

Celebrations were usually held in the community's heartland in Noor Baug but it was too stuffy for my taste. Daddy was a member of the Radio Club at Apollo Bunder and the idea of a reception in the open, near the sea appealed to me. So, we held it there the day after the *nikah* and served soft drinks, juices and passed around nuts and dry fruits on a platter.

After the reception, we came home to Darshan Apartments on Malabar Hill, and I have never left since!

I was the first among my peers to get married, so my friends and cousins had no advice for the wedding night. My aunts and Mummy also left us to our own devices. Chotu was a bit experienced in the matter, but nervous to share a bed with someone he loved and respected. However, we built an intense physical intimacy that lasted us all our lives.

After the wedding came the challenge of assimilating into a new family and running a home. When we began courting, Chotu had the foresight to acquire three floors in Darshan Apartments on *pagdi* basis.

Dr. DJ Jussawalla, my father-in-law's oncologist, lived in the apartment building and he told Chotu that Kersi Cambata, who owned Eros Cinema at Churchgate station and later established Cambata Aviation, wanted to sell his apartments on the 9th, 10th and 11th floors. Chotu saw a golden opportunity that he just could not pass up.

So he went through Nana Chudasama, a man about town then who did some brokering on the side. Chotu must have anticipated a large family (he was one among nine siblings), and pieced together the princely sum of ₹1 lakh. It was a very bold step and everyone cautioned him against it since it was only renting and not buying the apartment.

I was all of 17 when I stepped into the largest apartment I had ever seen, each room still containing colonial furniture the Cambatas left behind. I just locked up the 9th floor to make things more manageable. The 11th floor had only one room with french windows opening out to the terrace. We set up a bar there and entertained in the evenings. Bit by bit, we cleared out all the old furniture and had contemporary pieces made by the iconic Kamdar.

We chose a round dining table so that we could talk over meals, and I was excited to design a chair with their Russian designer Primakoff. Its back curved down to the seat, and the round base was upholstered in black-and-white fabric. The armrests were also upholstered to the tips. It became a popular model for Kamdar, and they asked whether they could include it in their catalogue—it was christened the Sabira chair. We also got Burma teak closets that I use to this day; the only thing that has needed upgrading is the handle.

My wise Daddy grabbed Ganesh Pillai from the Bombay Gymkhana, saying, "My daughter is a baby; you run her household", and sent him to me as bearer. Ganesh wore a peaked white cap, and put me in the habit of making monthly food plans, daily and weekly lists, and maintaining an inventory. I still plan my day like this so that I don't meander from object to object.

Chotu was keen that I keep expanding my horizons even after marriage. I would go riding at the Amateur Riders' Club at the Mahalakshmi Racecourse a few times a week. He also pushed me into joining swimming classes at the Cricket Club of India because we had a pool at Darshan and at our home in Bhavnagar. However, I never took to water like the proverbial fish. He fancied himself quite the dancer and encouraged me to enroll in the Rui Rose school of dancing. Rui was a middle-aged man who wore a two-piece suit, his hair slicked back with pomade. He had a dancer's straight spine, a little moustache and well-shined shoes. He taught us to waltz, to do the foxtrot and the tango. When I would come home, Chotu and I would practise in our living room.

This was the era of Chubby Checkers and the Twist, and Chotu loved to jive. We spent many evenings bouncing away in the Other Room at the Ambassador Hotel, ending with a Steak Fernandes (served with a dill-ginger-cinnamon sauce, doused with cognac and flambéed).

The most fun in domesticity came while putting into practice everything I learnt in Switzerland—our table was set with candles every night and we always dressed for dinner. Chotu loved expanding his palate, so I would experiment with food—steaks with cheese on our raclette grill, fondue, grilled fish...

However, I really learned things the hard way. Initially, I did things inefficiently and wasted food. But I never went to my mother or mother-in-law for help, or came down hard on myself. "Shoot. Well, never mind. I'll just have to learn to do this," I would mumble under my breath.

After Aly was born, Chotu and I talked about inviting his mother to live on the 9th floor, since it was lying empty. As I lacked a maternal presence in my life, I just made Chotu's mother mine. And she in turn always took the lead in integrating me into the family by putting my feelings first.

My new husband had a routine: he would return from work in the evening and send his briefcase up to our apartment while he dropped in for a chat with his mother.

Now, I hadn't been waiting all day to talk to a briefcase! But I didn't want Chotu to be torn between his wife and mother. Instead, I would go down to the 9th floor in the evening and we would all talk about our day.

My mother-in-law, whom I called Ba, was a very warm and generous person, and realized I didn't want to create a rift in the family, which helped us forge a strong bond.

She was also very diplomatic. Whenever Chotu and I had a row, I would promptly go report it to her, knowing she would take my side. "You are not to talk to him," she would usually say. "Stay here with me downstairs. Let him be alone for a while and see how he feels about that."

I don't know if she thought I was right or did this so that I didn't feel outnumbered, but it always worked. Seeing that his wife and mother were a unit, Chotu would come apologize to us both.

On my side of the family, Daddy would do the same. "You are going to have to be on your own," he would say, "I'm going to side with Chotu to keep the peace. If you need me to give you strength, I'm here."

And he was right. Chotu would be buttered and chuffed, thinking, "See, your dad agrees with me."

Ba and I grew so close that when she got cancer, she wanted no one but me to take care of her as she underwent treatment in London. She wanted to bequeath her diamond bangles to me, but I requested one of her saris as a memento instead. I didn't want our bond to be tarnished by even the whiff of transaction. In her will, she decreed that I oversee the ceremonial bathing of her body after she passed on, which was the greatest honour.

To assimilate into my new family, I learnt that I didn't need to throw my opinion in people's faces to make myself heard. I did things their way, went along with their activities and traditions. It is not that I was without a will; I was just happy to walk through a new door to see where it led.

Chotu and his older sister, Zarina, were passionate about cards and that is when Dadima's words came back to haunt me. I really detested gambling and it was the one bone of contention in our relationship for many years of our marriage.

I knew I couldn't stop him by throwing a tantrum or forbidding him. Instead, I thought I could be a cautionary presence. I would grab a book, call for a coke, and sit at the card table in the club.

This is also how I began enjoying drinks after my third child. My father and Chotu would enjoy a tipple together; I thought that there is no point sitting and watching them. If you can't beat them, you have got to join them, as the saying goes. So Chotu poured me a whisky and since then I have always been a scotch drinker.

Gambling did come between us often. One night, after we had been married a few years, Chotu didn't come home till 4 am. When I heard the sound of the elevator, I quickly went to the living room so that he could see I had waited up. He told me he had lost a lot of money. "This is going to destroy our family," I wept.

Another time, when I was taking care of Ba in London, Chotu and Zubi went out to the casino. It was my birthday and I told him to bid on my birth number, 4.

When they came back, Chotu told me he regretted not doing as I said; the number won all night. A few days later, I let him know how hurt I was that he had chosen gambling over spending time with me on my birthday, even as I nursed his mother.

I never demanded or expected an apology. I knew I would get it later, a hundred times over, if only I learnt to give in order to receive. I also felt that when it came to these habits, if I resisted, complained or fought to have my way, I would end up a lonely, bitter, old woman. If I wanted something, I would never approach it in the heat of the moment. Especially with my husband. Two days later, when the moment was light, I would tread the topic saying, "If you don't mind, shall we try it my way? But only if you don't mind. Otherwise, we can do it your way." He would not be able to refuse because I had asked so kindly and sweetly. And slowly, when Chotu could see the gambling was getting out of control, he gave it up.

Waiting patiently to make my point was also how I won the battle of the fuchsia sofa! When we were decorating the house in the 1960s, I wanted these modern Scandinavian triangular chairs. I imagined really violent colours playing against each other—a deep, deep golden carpet, which was quite a risk in those days as people came in with their dirty slippers, grey and golden thick *tussar* curtains and purple chairs. Laila Talukdar's lesson in thrilling colours had come back to me.

Chotu kept saying, "No, it's too much colour." I countered that we should add a little bit of pizzazz in our life, and asked him to give it a try. If he didn't like it, we could always tone it down. In those days, architect and Member of Parliament Piloo Mody (Sir Homi Mody's son) and his American wife Vina influenced my style greatly. I told Vina about the purple chairs and she jumped at the idea. "Purple it must be," she said. Then I decided—I must have been crazy—that the sofa should be fuschsia. I bought some fabric from Bharat Furnishing, threw it on the carpet and said, "Look how startling it looks!"

Everyone who walked into the house would say, "Ah God, this is really something." It could have been right out of an *Architectural Digest.* I eventually grew into muted shades and currently live in an all-white home. But when you are in your 20s, you want to explore and make a statement.

Piloo and Vina also helped us with the nursery. We had beige curtains with the alphabet on them in applique. We started out with a bed for Aly with padded rexine on the sides so that he wouldn't hurt himself if he rolled into them. When Heena came along, they adapted it into a bunk bed. When Saleem popped up after that, they added a pull-out drawer in the lower bed and said, "That is all we can do. This better be the last baby you have!"

The way the couple mounted their art collection also made a lasting impression on me. The welcome area in their Altamount Road bungalow was an expansive circular room. In the centre of this lobby, carved and faceted chains—thick enough to hold down elephants—were suspended from the ceiling and dropped down to a circle of pants. The walls were covered with paintings. The overall effect was so immersive that I decided I would also like to have art take over our rooms. Vina founded one of the country's first lifestyle stores, Contemporary Arts & Craft, which is her lasting Valentine to homegrown crafts. When she passed away in August 2021, she left behind a legacy that keeps our heritage skills relevant in homes and daily life.

When I started collecting art, only with the intent of enjoying it, I slowly changed the decor around it. Currently, the upholstery and artefacts in my sitting room are white and silver, to accentuate MF Husain's white horses on the wall. Similarly, the dining area has accents of rust and terracotta spilling over from the large Laxman Shrestha facing the dining table. I bought paintings and sculptures for a few thousand rupees and over the years, this has grown into a legacy I take pride in. It has also piqued the interest of auction houses such as Sotheby's.

Eventually, in the '70s, we built the apartment on the 11th floor in which we currently live. There was a closed bid for the terrace above our apartment and Chotu's was the highest. We decided to move our living quarters to this new space. Eventually, our sons and their families took up the 10th floor.

Chotu and I had similar ideas on what we wanted the home to look like—slanting, high ceiling. I had seen *My Fair Lady* on my first visit to London, and a winding staircase leading to a library on the mezzanine was imprinted in my mind. I also wanted a terrace with a fountain.

We tried a few architects and none of them worked out. When we heard that the Italian architect Eugenio

Montuori was in town, I wrangled an introduction. He had designed the Rome Train Terminus and was here for the Trombay Research Centre. I begged him to take up our assignment, and he agreed because he saw the potential. It was one of the few residences he designed in Southeast Asia. He collaborated with a local architect, Sam Rao. They would correspond over post, sending letters and plans across continents using snail mail.

Montuori was very particular about acoustics and we moved to the neighbouring Everest Apartments for a year and a half while he blew up the place a few times to get it just right. He could not stand the noise bouncing off the walls and ceiling. Then he put in large sliding windows, unheard of in those days, which flooded the apartment with space and light. He was very pleased with the result and the apartment looks modern even today. Visitors say they feel like they have walked into a living space in New York.

The Modys and Montuori were just some of the people who shaped my taste and furthered my education after Switzerland. Moving to South Bombay opened a whole new world of sophistication to this Bandra babe.

Lady Soonu Jeejeebhoy's friendship introduced me to Bombay's upper crust. Soonu knew me fleetingly as she was earlier married to Naval Tata, my father's best friend. She inducted me into her organisation, Women Emergency Welfare Organisation (WEWO), to "infuse fresh blood into it".

The meetings were held at Sett Minar, the Jeejeebhoy mansion on Peddar Road, which was such an institution that it didn't even have a number to mark it. Liveried footmen in white glided soundlessly, circulating smoked salmon or *akuri* on toast. The tablecloth and napkins were made of organdie or starched linen and hand embroidered by nuns in convents. Everywhere one looked, there were daily implements made of silver—ashtrays, vases, cutlery, ladles. Even the soap dish in the guest bathroom was made of the precious metal.

I was in the company of the most elegant and esteemed women of the city—Silloo Maoji, Shirin Petigara, Nergish Nariman and Maki Commissariat. Many of them were in their 50s, and the servers, mistaking me for a 'baby' and not a 'madam', would pass me over when serving alcohol! Ratan Tata, then a young man (he is just a few years older than me) would stop to greet us sometimes. Even then, his politeness and courteousness set him apart from other men his age.

On the home front, Chotu and I were welded together by our excitement to share everything with each other. We would talk about literally anything, and our minds became the driving factors in our marriage.

Though I was never a very sporty person, if a cricket match was going on I would read the papers so that I could chat with him about it. Seeing that I was interested in business, he would tell me his plans. He liked an inquiring mind, and reciprocated by learning more about things I was interested in, such as theatre and the arts. Our communication grew manifold by just loving and learning through that love.

But that was just the foundation.

Chotu's romantic ways sweetened every day we spent together. He would find small, considerate ways of showing how grateful he was for all that I did for him and the family, such as wrapping two strings of *mogra* around my wrists just because he saw them at the traffic lights and thought of me. Or bringing home tickets to the theatre or a musical evening.

He also became very creative at giving gifts, but that could be because of the row we had on my 18th birthday. Chotu had some work in Birmingham and I decided to tag along; it became our maiden trip abroad as a couple. We were in London for my first birthday after marriage, and Chotu gave me cash in an envelope. "What kind of a woman do you think I am?" I said, flinging it at him. After that, almost every gift came wrapped in a surprise.

Once in London, he came back from a jaunt and threw a crumpled piece of tissue on the bed. "Hey," I asked, "what's this?" It turned out to be a beautiful thick entwined rope of gold he had seen in Hatton Garden and felt Sabi must have. I slipped it on right then as we went out for the evening.

Another time, he slipped in a diamond among ice cubes in a glass and told me to look carefully before I poured. During the Studio 29 days, he bought me a pendant that looked like a raw gold nugget with little diamonds.

My husband's most important rule was 'Sabi must have jewellery' and he became very good at choosing, commissioning and pursuing pieces in partnership with the family jeweller Hirabhai. Almost every ornament I own is a gift from him, and he would love to see me wearing them. Even in the last days, when we were in and out of hospitals, he would remind me that I needed to change my accessories. I told him I couldn't be bothered to go to the bank locker to take things out, but he would insist.

One of my most treasured gifts is a Bird of Paradise brooch. He had seen a photograph of it in a magazine; it had won an international jewellery design award. The bird was made entirely of diamond baguettes and had a pearl hanging from its beak. It took him nearly two years to amass the perfect gemstones to replicate the undulation of the bird's wing. Hirabhai patiently set it in wax, got Chotu's nod and finalized it in platinum.

Though he bought me baubles all the time, he would especially get me a piece when he made some money. It was, of course, good investment, but also his way of sharing his success with me.

Once, the business faced some financial setback. And what did Chotu do? He went out to Rayne's, shoemakers to the Queen of England, and splurged on shoes and bags for me. "Why are you doing this?" I wept. He simply shrugged and said, "I wanted to feel good."

In the later years, being in a wheelchair could not deter him. We were window shopping in Hong Kong once and saw a limited-edition Versace bag that I loved but found too dear. It was crafted out of Chinese silk, bearing a dragon motif to commemorate the Year of the Dragon, with large beads of lapis hanging from the thick gold links. When I stepped out to get my hair done, Chotu made the nurse spin his wheelchair around and head straight to the store to buy it! It is now in the front in my closet so I can see it often.

He was one of those rare men who gave his wife his full attention: I could not step outside the house without passing his inspection. He would make me twirl slowly, review my ensemble and make additions or subtract the accessories. Even as his health deteriorated in his 80s, which meant I increasingly went out alone, I could not escape his scanner.

His frequent suggestion was that I wear higher heels because shoes were his passion just like they were mine, and I would have to remind him I was no longer 35 years old.

I would do the same for him: buying him silk ties and pocket squares, helping him choose and coordinate when we went out. When we gave each other our full attention, it felt like we were going out as a team.

After more than 55 years together, young people often asked me the secret to our marriage. Apart from shared values and vision and just fitting well together, my practical advice would be to never share bathrooms. You just don't need to see each other's mess!

Our bathrooms were first separated by the shower area, so we could still talk to each other. Later, when we moved to the 11th floor, he put a chair in his bathroom so that we could chat while he shaved. It was an intimate gesture he inherited from his parents.

Kaka, my father-in-law, wanted Ba to be an integral part of his life. He had a beautiful big bathroom with heated rods for towels. He installed a large armchair for Ba so that they could jabber while he tended to his appearance. She was very wise with a lot of common sense and emotional intelligence. Both of them were not highly educated, but informed and instinctive. I suppose such a strong and deep parental unit set an ideal for Chotu and he absorbed the importance of cultivating it.

As exciting as it was to get gifts and enjoy evenings out, I also knew to do without them and to not expect or demand them.

A few years into our marriage, before the children were of schoolgoing age, we had to move our family to the Merchants' hometown Bhavnagar, in Gujarat. The family's fortune was built on turning groundnuts into *vanaspati*, a crucial cooking medium from the 1940s to the 1970s.

Bhavnagar Vegetable Products produced Prabhat Vanaspati, the second leader in the market after Dalda. It was a company Chotu's father, Abdul Hussein Ghulam Hussein, had built from scratch. My father-in-law was a force to reckon with and had an acumen which very few people possessed.

He would go into the fields, feel the soil and predict what the next monsoon, and thus the crop, would be like. He would then wager whether the market would go up or down and be a forward buyer. There was a big element of gambling to this, but Kaka was seldom wrong. He grew his father Ghulam Hussein's small oil mill into such an empire that, it was said, even the Maharaja of Bhavnagar envied him.

The glittering jewel of his success was the house he built in Majirajwadi. A long winding driveway led to the one-story house with a pool at the back, which was just a cemented tank. There were seven bedrooms with marble floors, all air-conditioned centrally by a gigantic unit that squatted at the back. A *jhula* in the middle of the house, between the living room and the kitchen, was Ba's seat from where she ran the home.

Chotu would tell me what a single-minded and amazing person Kaka was, just like his father before him. He learnt to drive in one single night—he borrowed someone's car and went out in the field and practised turns and reversed. He even got under the bonnet to understand how the engine worked.

Kaka arranged his own wedding, an uncommon act of independence in those times. With what little money he had, he bought himself a pair of burgundy velvet embroidered shoes for the ceremony. But he stepped into a puddle as soon as he left his house and the colour bled. He was terribly upset. "The one beautiful thing I had in my life that I could show my wife..." he cried.

Kaka was also very generous, which I think Chotu imbibed. He was so grateful to Dr. Manilal Shah in Bhavnagar—who nursed him through his first cancer—that he gifted him a beige Fiat.

Chotu and his two brothers—Mamu and Nisar—inherited the business after their father died in his 50s. However, by the late '60s, it wasn't doing so well. Vanaspati was no longer a popular cooking medium, and the company began to lose money. Chotu thought we could make a difference by moving to Bhavnagar and being involved in the day-to-day running of the factory.

The children were still young, so it was easy for us to shift homes. Bhavnagar was a provincial town with only the Maharaja, and the chief banker of the State Bank of India, Mr. Puri, comprising high society. The club was just a teeny establishment where men went to play cards; nothing to visit as a couple.

Among Chotu's handful of friends was Antu. He worked for an insurance company and would come over in the evenings to play rummy or poker, while the cook rustled up dinner and drinks.

Food was mainly vegetarian, and I missed my fish dearly. But instead of moping around, I used my time to learn Gujarati cooking and to speak the language fluently. I had already picked up a little from Ba, but I wanted to speak it better. So, Antu's wife and I would converse only in Gujarati, which brought me closer to Chotu's sisters. Hanging around Antu's home, I learnt to make *khandvi*, *bhaat* and other local delicacies.

Since my regular Bombay frocks and skirts would not do, I went shopping for cotton block-printed saris and salwar suits, and had great fun designing blouses (it never occurred to me to wear sleeveless ones, even though it was a hundred degrees). My hair then was a flicked-out bob, a la Jackie Kennedy.

I remember one Diwali, my American sister-in-law Mary became quite the spectacle in a silk skirt suit and high heels. The festival was grandly celebrated in our Bhavnagar home and everyone would come with flowers and *mithai* for Ba. The visitors were scandalized to see my sister-in-law's knees and kept staring at her.

Being a voracious reader, books became a beloved pastime while the children splashed about in the pool. There were a few lying around the house, but I would also bring back magazines such as *Time*, *Newsweek*, *India Today*, bestselling novels or *Reader's Digest*s from our trips to Bombay.

Excitement came in the form of guests from out of town. The architect Charles Correa came over often. His wife Monica had studied with Chotu's sister Zubi and one of his first projects was a pair of bungalows in Bhavnagar coincidentally commissioned by Chotu's cousins Mammu-bhai and Abdi-bhai. The former was also married to Chotu's sister Roshan.

They were two extremely modern, pure white bungalows in Hill Drive, built to be reflections of each other. Inside, every room was on a split level. The homes were called The Twins and coincidentally, Mallika—Abdi's wife—also gave birth to twins.

Our daily involvement in the family business was not helping; every day Chotu would come home with depressing news. We had to fight just to keep our heads above water, but it nourished our marriage. Chotu was no longer his gregarious self—there were no more surprise baubles or dinners, but I didn't mind. The children and I found ways to lighten his burden.

The one thing I put my foot down for was the gambling aspect of the trade. My husband and his brothers did not inherit their father's acumen and instinct for predicting the market, and it was not something that could be cultivated.

Much of their business in Bhavnagar involved wagering on the future harvest of oil seeds, which they would then either sell or buy. The prediction of the monsoon and thus the harvest was not easy and this was a point of discontent between us. I would beg him to stick to the actual manufacturing so that we didn't lose everything.

In the end, after a couple of years or so, when Chotu summed up the figures, he saw that we were not making much of a difference by living in Bhavnagar. He spoke to Ba and told her that we had decided to come back to Bombay.

Around the time that Prabhat Vanaspati was dissolving, my father's business was also going through a churn.

His company, Vazir Glass Works, first produced soda bottles, the kind sealed by marbles which you would push down to drink from. He supplied them to Dukes and Rogers, the two big cold drink manufacturers of the time. Then, he branched out into glass vials that would be used for injectables, nose and ear drops. Pfizer and all the other major pharmaceutical companies were his clients.

His factory was in Andheri and the government was clearing the area to build a highway, which meant it would be knocked down. They offered my father a pittance for the space, and the cost of relocation and setting up the factory again while continuing servicing our clients was daunting. My father was in frail health that year—he had already been through a few mild heart attacks—and was looking for new financial partners.

A British company called the Bombay Company came forth and my father talked it over with Chotu. He knew he needed the money they were offering, but was afraid that the investors would take over and leave him as only a figurehead.

Chotu thought about it very deeply and said to me, "Do you think my brothers and I should make a consortium and put in the money with your dad and get into this business?"

I was very wary because here was my father, whom I loved so much, and on the other hand was my husband. Say there was a financial clash, what would happen? I was protective of my father, but I did want Chotu to partner with him because I was afraid the British investors would dislodge Daddy. The fact was that my father could not see beyond Chotu.

It so happened that everything worked out for the best. All the new partners—Chotu and his brothers—agreed that my father would be the company's chairman and the main person behind the factory. Later, the Shahs, sons of Kaka's partner Gambhir Bhai, also joined the business. It turned into a long association when Gambhir-bhai's son, Bhailal, took over the reins from his father. Bhailal's son, Hemant Shah, is still a director of Vazir Glass Works.

With the infusion of fresh funds we could order better equipment such as fully automatic Individual Section (IS) machines and service our clients better. When we came back to Bombay, Vazir Glass Works started a new era. It eventually became Chotu's main business and he renamed it Neutral Glass Works. He also ran a hire-purchase business, ANCO, with his partner Jawahar Parekh.

The new factory was around where JW Marriott now stands in Andheri and Chotu kept buying adjoining lots of land, for, as he liked to say, the amount I spent on my ribbons. Soon we had about 11 acres.

Facing labour troubles, Chotu and his partners elected to move the factory to Kosumba in Gujarat in the early '80s. He sold it only in 2014 to a German company when he planned his retirement.

Eventually, we sold the Bhavnagar home too and it was razed to the ground to build a multi-storey building. It now exists only in my thoughts and memories.

Through all the ups and downs of our circumstances, Chotu and I held on to each other. We raised our children, cherished our grandchildren, and enjoyed a long and fulfilling retirement. No matter how high I soared professionally, he never begrudged me my success. Instead, he was always pushing me to the forefront, encouraging me to take on new challenges, attending the first show of every play and letting me know with a discreet cough that he was in the audience.

Many people say their relationship is cemented by their children, but Chotu and I were conjoined only by our love for each other, and our family came through that love.

4

Family, the Centre of Everything

EVERYTHING PIVOTS AROUND THE family. As much as our three children cemented our relationship, Chotu and I, to be candid, didn't need them to hold us together. We were a unit unto ourselves.

In the 1950s and '60s, one did not talk about children or plan their arrival. Once you got married, the outcome was children. And everyone wanted three or more.

As soon as I got married, I got caught up in the whirlwind of domesticity—managing a multi-storey home, learning a new language and acclimatising to a new culture (Chotu's family spoke in Gujarati at home and kept up with some Bhavnagri traditions), fitting into a large new family of six sisters, five of whom were married, and two brothers and their respective partners, not to mention my mother-in-law.

By the time our first anniversary came around on February 25, 1961, I was heavily pregnant. A few weeks later, at the age of 18, I gave birth to Aly and barrelled into adulthood and motherhood together. Heena came soon after in 1963, and that was the number of children we wanted. In 1964, before I could get out of my maternity clothes, Saleem popped up.

I was constantly pregnant from ages 17 to 21, and since I was such a slight girl, I carried all the weight in the front. My belly looked like the nose of a Boeing plane and for all those years I couldn't see my toes. It became a game at parties to see how many cups of coffee I could balance on my belly (two!).

With Saleem, it was the end of Mummy-game for me, and Chotu very wisely came forward to have a vasectomy. This was unheard of at the time but he was wary of the side effects of the pill. He had no qualms that the procedure would affect his manhood or prowess.

We wanted short and simple names for the children—'Aly' just sounded nice and my mother-in-law approved because of the religious connotations; I liked 'Heena' and had a close cousin by that name. I thought it would be a nice double connection to be able to think of my beloved cousin whenever I called my daughter's name. Saleem shares his name with my elder brother, who took care of the family after Bapaji. Like our father, he had a finely-tuned moral compass and tethered me to my family in Pakistan after my biological parents passed away.

These days, my children have taken on different roles. Our youngest child Saleem, whom we used to despair about because he ran away from boarding school so often, has taken on the role of my father after Chotu's demise. He calls me three times a day to see if I need anything, invites himself over for meals or just coffee, and reprimands me if he hears that I have taken a cab to church instead of asking for his car and driver. He even keeps a tab on my comings and goings through the staff!

Heena, my middle child and only daughter, has grown into my soulmate. She lives in America, but we try to see each other twice a year—I go over for three to four weeks, and she tries to come down to Mumbai too. She was the first of our children to have kids and this brought us even closer. We cherish walking around New York City together. Sometimes she sleeps over in my hotel room and we get uninterrupted quality time.

Aly, our firstborn, remained my child till the very end. He struggled with depression right from school. Chotu's family had a strain of mental illness and it cost his sister Zarina her life. Aly passed away shortly after his father in 2017.

In his last years, though Aly lived separately, I ran his home for him—sent him his meals, had his laundry brought over every day, saw to the maintenance of his house and even hired and trained his staff. A nurse-cum-companion lived with him to ensure there was some human interaction and it fell upon me to remind the brother to give Aly his medication, push him to go for a walk or just coax him, in a hundred different ways, to interact with the outside world.

He was such a pretty and happy baby. As with any first-time parents, we were excited about his arrival. Chotu insisted we buy a few things for our firstborn from Harrods since we were in London when I was pregnant. The luxury department store had an 'Italy at Harrod's' festival, showcasing beautiful things by Italian designers.

"Should we go for white or yellow?" asked Chotu, aiming for gender neutrality. "Blue!" I said firmly, "Because we're going to have a son."

"How can you be so sure?"

"Come on! I have been to the homes of so many couples and they all had sons. My brother was born after I came in. It has to be a boy!" I said, referring to my 'fertility charm'.

"I've never seen someone so sure of anything in their life," Chotu said, throwing in the towel. "Let's get everything in blue."

So, we bought for our first child some blue clothes and the softest eiderdown made of blue silk and stuffed with 'modern' synthetic fibres that were light unlike the goose down we used then. Our prized purchase was a beautiful brass collapsible cot that had silk cords at the trellis so that the baby's feet would not be hurt when he hit it. We also bought a ceramic lamp that is still with me. It became part of the children's landscape as they grew up and Heena is so emotionally attached to it that she often reminds me, "If anything happens to you, Mummy, I'm taking that lamp!"

Fortuitously, my brother's teacher, Mr. Rowe, was shifting his residence from England to India around the same time we were shopping for the nursery, and we requested him to carry all our things in the cargo.

All the children gave us hints of what their personalities would be like as they started going to school. Or rather, even as they came into the world.

With Aly, I was in labour for four days and was sent

back from the hospital twice. Finally, the doctor said he would have to induce birth or we would have to have a caesarean. The thought of being cut up scared me so much that I pushed with all my might, and along came Aly. I also nursed him the longest—nine months. He was a reluctant feeder, falling asleep while drawing. I would have to pat his cheeks or mop his face with a wet towel to wake him to start drinking again. Sometimes the nurse would take off all his clothes so that he would emerge from his slumber when he felt cold. He always remained reluctant to engage with life.

Heena was 'Little Miss Independent' the moment she drew her first breath of air. In the seventh month of my second pregnancy, I got the measles. My face was so swollen that my eyes were closed shut. I was burning up with 104–105° F fever. We were all worried about how this might affect the foetus or complicate the pregnancy. My mother-in-law sent me her maid who would keep applying cold compresses on my tummy, neck, chest and forehead to bring down the fever. Luckily, both the baby and I got through the illness safely, and Heena never contracted measles because of the immunity she had built in the womb.

When I went into labour, Dr. Saraiya, who was overseeing the delivery, said I hadn't dilated enough and went for lunch. The young nurse too stepped out for a break and I rapidly slipped into labour! The bell was too far for me to reach when Heena decided to make her entrance! When the nurse popped in to see whether I wanted some tea, she saw an infant attached to the umbilical cord, wriggling in the afterbirth, playing with my toes!

The sister must have been new to the profession for she panicked. It fell upon me to coach her on how to massage my stomach so that the body could expunge the placenta lest it became toxic. She caught hold of an on-duty doctor who cut off the umbilical cord and cleaned up the afterbirth. By the time Dr. Saraiya came back from lunch, I had a gurgling baby in my arms.

Saleem's birth was indicative of all the excitement he was to bring into our lives! Chotu was at the hospital in the morning when I went into labour, but was called away because there was a surprise check at his office on Sir PM Road. The baby's head was so large that I was badly lacerated and lost a lot of blood. The doctors advised a transfusion to make up for the loss but I flatly refused. I had read and heard so much about the complications after the procedure that I preferred to repair on my own.

When Chotu came to see me and the baby in the evening, he was wearing the day's worries on his face and the marks from the morning's trials on his arms (I had held his arm so tightly during labour that it had left bruises).

It was our friend Malti 'Malu' Divecha's birthday and she was throwing a barbecue party on her terrace. I forced Chotu to go knowing it would do him good to meet some friends. The day's highs and lows—the extreme excitement of welcoming a new baby and the exhaustion of dealing with authorities—were so overwhelming that he says that was one of the few times he got completely drunk.

Saleem was also unique for the fact that of all my children, he was the only one to not speak in English. He communicated purely in Hindi till he was two years old, and then one fine day, he just snapped out of it and switched to English.

As soon as Aly was born, Chotu started planning for his future. "We might as well start thinking of schools," he said, even before the baby and I were discharged from Breach Candy Hospital. We had spoken about The Cathedral and John Connon School, and Chotu brought the registration forms to the hospital!

All the children were born at Breach Candy Hospital which had a British pre- and post-natal specialist called Dr. Moos. She had coached me while I was pregnant and gave me exercises to do after delivery. I had 16 stitches after Aly's birth, but she was pitiless. "Bring her tightest dress when you come to see her next," she instructed Chotu.

He brought my brown wiggle dress with flowers on it, which she made me squeeze into and look at myself in the mirror. Of course, I looked ghastly with bulges everywhere. "Now," she commanded, "you are going to fit into this in three months." It was her way of motivating me to do all the exercises and I credit her for teaching me the importance of following a fitness regimen all my life.

No family member came to stay with me during my pregnancies or after the babies were born. A nurse called

Maria came home from the hospital. I knew I had her only for three months, so I quickly learnt to bathe, feed and change nappies from her. Then came the task of running a home and, eventually, looking after the children while being a teenager myself.

Later came Flory who helped us look after Heena, and Tulsi, whom Saleem loved to death. Our bearer and major-domo, Ganesh, was also a favourite with the children because of how much he made them laugh.

When Aly was about two months old, he got very ill and we requested Dr. Merchant, who had a roaring practice in the area, to come take a look at him. I wasn't feeling too well and was lying on the sofa in my grey-blue dressing gown when the doorbell rang. The good doctor strode in, sat next to me, took my pulse and asked me how I was feeling. "Fine, just a bit tired," I replied. "It's all right, your mother has called me to look after you," Dr. Merchant said. "No, no, no," I said alarmed, "I rang you up to see my son." "You have a son?" he said. "But you are a child yourself."

Just then, Chotu walked in and Dr. Merchant turned on him saying, "Are you the man who has given this child a baby?" "Yes, so what?" my husband said, "she's not a child. She's 18!" I suppose I looked like I was 15 because I had a round, chubby face!

Eventually, Dr. Merchant became a family friend and took me through the other two pregnancies and became the pediatrician to all our children.

Chotu was very busy setting up our lives and providing for the family, and couldn't be involved with the burping and bathing of the babies. "You bring up the children the way you want to bring them up," he said. "But what do I know about parenting? Zero!" "Well then, just bring them up the best you can," he said. So, I read books on mothering and parenting. Chotu also gave me a book called *The Ideal Marriage* by Dutch gynecologist Theodoor Hendrik van de Velde, which I read from cover to cover.

Our biggest task was drying out cloth diapers during the monsoons—there were no disposable ones in those days. I don't know why, but I never turned to my mother-in-law or mother for help or advice regarding the little ones. Nobody came to stay the nights when they were ill; I guess they were confident that I could handle it on my own.

As they grew up, the children brought into our lives a whole new set of friends. Gobind and Patsy (Patricia) lived together on the second floor when I first got pregnant. Elevators in residential buildings were a fairly uncommon feature then and ours used to stop working very often. I would lumber up to the 10th floor with my Boeing belly. Patsy and Gobind kindly kept a chair outside their door for me to rest. Their first child Ayesha was the same age as Heena. Then came Jean and Rustom Cambata from the eighth floor and their kids Anita, Mehra, Tina and Shahrookh. Through the Cambatas, we met Jaishree and Rajan Mittal, and Leena, Medha, Nandita and Radhika whose ages coincided with that of my children. The Cambatas also introduced us to Malu and Bhagwan Divecha, and their son Arjun, who was slightly older than Aly. We also became friendly with Bobby and Maheen Rawjee through their children Riyaz and Shabbir.

Through Malu, we made the acquaintance of Harish and Indira Mahindra, and their children Anand, Anuja and Radhika. Even at a young age, Anand stood out as an articulate boy who thought before he spoke and chose words carefully. He went on to study in Ooty, and we met him when we were there on holiday. Children in boarding schools look forward to an outing, so we treated him and his friend to lunch at the iconic Chinese restaurant, Shinkows.

All of these children grew up together, going to play downstairs with their maids, eating in each other's houses. Shahrookh, for years, subsisted only on Irish Stew and scrambled eggs and refused to eat anything else at our house.

The Cambatas had a gem of a preview theatre above Eros Cinema. It seated about 60 people and was plush with red carpets, seats you could sink into and Art Deco details. Every so often, we would drive over in Chotu's white and canyon tan Plymouth and gather with our friends to watch *Cheaper by the Dozen* or *Where Eagles Dare* before it hit the theatres. Afterwards, we would all go to each other's place for potluck dinner.

The memory of one parenting incident still fills me with remorse. Chotu and I were headed to a movie and the children and their maids were in the car with us. We told them we would meet them later and they misunderstood that to mean that they should wait in the parking lot outside Eros Cinema! When we came back hours later to find them waiting in a closed car, I was extremely distressed.

Chotu made some wonderful memories with the children in Bhavnagar. There weren't any other children to play with there, so Chotu and I became their playmates. He and Heena would knock almonds off trees with stones and sit on the big green swing inside the house and tell stories. He was a great storyteller and would leave Heena asking for more. "And then what happened, daddy?" was her constant refrain.

A major activity for the children there was to bob about in our painted cement 'pool'. I didn't enjoy the water so much, but the children and Chotu were always splashing about. They would also play games like 'kick the can'.

Our evening outings were to the lake called Bor Talao, located in the centre of town. It had a paved promenade around the periphery and we would go along munching *seeng-chana* (roasted peanuts and pulses). On some days, to make it fun for the kids, we would ride there on a bullock cart and wave to everyone on our way.

A departure from routine came in the form of our friends from Bombay. Jean and Russi Cambata visited us a few times, once even with Jean's parents from Sheffield. All the kids—ours and theirs—put up a play for us. The idea came from something I was reading (the home had a large library) or a historical event.

We had a small *chowki* where the *chowkidaar* lived and this was turned into a stage. We sat around with our drinks and some hot *bhajiyas*, watching the plot unfold.

When we moved back to Bombay, it was time to enrol the children in school. Chotu, the Papa Bear, was minutely involved in their education, right up to after college.

We—the children and I—signed up for Westwind Nursery, which is a starter school for those who want to get into Cathedral. It's run by the mothers of the students as a sort of collective effort, and I offered to help with either the activities or dramatics—anything that didn't involve numbers.

The children's personalities also came through when it was time to go to school—Aly was indifferent; Heena was self-assured and matter-of-fact. She just decided that she was going to have a good time with her friends and would hurry off without turning back even once. Saleem had the hardest time adjusting. He cried so much that the long-standing principal, Roshan Curmally, made an exception and let Tulsi, our maid whom Saleem was very attached to, sit on a chair outside the classroom for a whole week till he slipped into the routine.

As the children grew up, Chotu became keen that they go to a boarding school to learn to be independent. He didn't want maids and ayahs to do everything for them. It was an expensive proposition but it meant so much to Chotu that he took a loan from his business associates to send them off to England.

About the time they turned nine and ten, we began scouting for residential schools. Aly, being the eldest, was the first to go. Saleem followed him to Mayo College in Ajmer for a year or so to ease into a life away from home, before they both went abroad.

While Aly expressed his unhappiness but reluctantly accepted this new reality, Saleem remained homesick for a long time.

Eventually, Aly went to Charter House in Surrey, while Saleem progressed to Hawkhurst Court Prep School. It was in residential schools Aly's clinical depression first manifested. His housemaster reported that he was very lonely and would not mix with the other students. We consulted a few psychiatrists who diagnosed him and prescribed medication. To ease the regimented life of a residential school, we arrived at an arrangement with Pearl Sayed who, coincidentally, was related to my best friend Pearl Padamsee. Aly would go live with her on the odd weekend or short holiday because a homey atmosphere would do him good.

Heena went directly to St. Michael's, Burton Park, and though she didn't like the thought of living away from home at first, she settled in quickly. She is open to new experiences and her letters were cheerful with always a mention of food.

All the children came back home to Bombay in their late teens. Heena moved to America later to study and settled there. She gave birth to two boys—Arjun in 1990 and Armaan in 1992, and helping her with motherhood brought us closer together.

Co-incidentally, Saleem married Tayunaz Engineer, daughter of my school friend Katayun, and her husband Cyrus Engineer. Katy Baxter, as we called her in school, was one of the friends I would share tiffin with in recess. She was a year ahead, and I was so happy to reconnect with her.

Tayunaz was three years behind Saleem in John Cannon and Cathedral School, while her brother Shahrokh was a year ahead of him, and in class with Heena. We all moved in the same circles, and Shahrokh and Saleem became friends. Later, Tayunaz and Saleem fell in love and got married in 1989.

She is a very gentle, warm, sweet and unassuming girl who integrated into our family smoothly. She is very well-brought up and there has never been a cross word between us in all these years. She is a magician in the kitchen, and I look forward to meals at their house. Give her five ingredients and she will conjure up something unpredictable and delightful. She is also very enterprising and has turned her passion into a profession—she teaches others to cook various kinds of cuisine.

I named Saleem and Tayunaz's sons—Azhaan and Zarvaan--and they are the grandchildren I saw the most due to proximity. They are both adults now, on their individual paths; Azhaan in London and Zarvaan in Dubai. Both the boys are polite and well-mannered, and a credit to their parents.

Aly fell in love with a Punjabi girl, Ritu, who was the daughter of a chocolate-making partner from when I turned entrepreneur and ran Giftique. I had my reservations about him getting married as I didn't think he was ready to take responsibility for another person. However, Chotu thought the responsibility would steer Aly into a balanced life. They have a son, Kabir, and our only granddaughter, Kareena. At six feet four inches, Kabir is the tallest of our grandchildren. Kareena is studying to be a pediatrician in Bengaluru and will be the most qualified of the next generation of Merchants.

For a long time, we all lived as one big joint family in Darshan Apartments, except for Heena and her husband Dhananjay Pai, who live in New York.

Eventually, I just could not manage the household. Aly and Ritu were going their separate ways, and I had to convince Chotu—even though I knew it would break his heart—to sell the 10th floor so that we could give the children their own homes. The brick-and-mortar unit represented family life to Chotu, since it was the home we had started our married life in and the one he had brought his mother into to take care of her.

But it had to be done. Anticipating Aly's dependence on me, we bought him an apartment close by, and were able to set Ritu and the children up in a nice flat in Bengaluru. Saleem's family moved to Breach Candy, where they still live.

When Chotu passed away, I invited all the grandchildren to help themselves to scarves, berets and ties from his wardrobe so that they would have something to remember him by.

5

My Days as Bombay's Quiz Queen

BY THE TIME I was 21, I had had three children and was restive. "This is not the only thing I want in life," I thought to myself. Mind you, in the early '60s, it was quite sufficient to be just a mother and a homemaker. Your husband went out to earn a living, you went out to social events, joined ladies' clubs, helped in your children's school and gave your time to charities. Why would you want to be anything else?

I was introduced to Adi Marzban at a party and he immediately said, "You speak so well; why don't we try you out on radio?" And thus began a long, fulfilling public life.

Adi Marzban is among the people the Parsis are possessively proud of. And rightly so. Adi was a creative dynamo—he was the editor of *Jam-e-Jamshed*, the periodical for the Indian Zoroastrian diaspora; wrote and produced plays in Gujarati; adapted plays from English for the Indian audience; and was producing some shows for All India Radio. He has written on every aspect of the human condition and his plays are still being performed or adapted today.

First, I became a part of a live programme that was simply called *An Evening at All India Radio*. I was on air seven to ten nights in a row and I took it on because it fit with my lifestyle. I was able to tuck the children into bed and work while they were sleeping.

The programme was mainly about the lives of people who were of creative value in the Western world, such as Beethoven, Brahms, the Brontë sisters and many other musical and literary stalwarts. Adi would research their lives and work, script a radio play and direct us. It was a show that all the expats, Parsis and Christians of Bombay—anyone with a European tilt—would tune into.

We would leave home at 7.30 or 8 pm to go to the studios at Churchgate where we would be handed sheets of paper containing the script and dialogue. We would have a quick rehearsal and go live by 9–9.30 pm.

Adi would sit on the console behind a sheet of glass like a conductor to operate the voice level, clarity, music, and signal to speak louder or higher, and fade out.

On our part, we would be very careful to slip the sheets of paper noiselessly on the floor as we finished reading them. It was crucial that this didn't make any sound that could be caught by the microphone. At the end of the play, the floor would be covered with pages.

Adi and I went on to work for nearly a quarter of a century on TV, radio and theatre. He was a short man, usually in a shirt and pair of trousers that looked like he had slept in them... and he probably had. He was so lost in creativity that he would forget mortal rituals such as sleeping and bathing. I can still see him walking about with a lit cigarette, ash staggering precariously until he absentmindedly found something to employ as an ashtray.

I would pick him up from his home on my way to the Doordarshan studios, packing a sandwich as lunch because he couldn't be bothered with something as dull as feeding himself. Often, he would forget to wear a belt and his trousers would trickle down as he stood. "Adi, don't you think you should run up and get it," I would say. "*Arré, kai nai* (oh, never mind)," he would say to brush it off, and then thread his *kushti*, the sacred thread Parsis wear, through the belt loops to hold up his pants!

His sweet wife Siloo would despair over his workaholic ways. He would work deep into the night, writing each play, script and article by hand in his Chapsi Terrace home on Altamount Road. The next morning, he would hand it to us in the form of a radio script, dialogue for a play or ideas for a TV show.

We put together a game game show called *Drawing You Out* on DD. It ran for about four episodes but didn't connect with the audience. A member of the participating team would be given a theme, which the person would draw out on the blackboard with coloured chalk. But the show was telecast in black and white. Once a team had to draw a bowl of spaghetti and it looked like a plate of worms. The audience just could not guess what it was.

Then he conceived *What's the Good Word* and in his typical mad scientist way left it to me to flesh it out. The concept of the game was seemingly simple: There were three contesting teams with two players each. Each team was given a stack of cards with a word written on them. One person from each team would draw a card simultaneously to take a look at the word, and then give clues to his or her partner about it. The clues could not be a non-English word, a proper noun, or rhyming word. For instance, if the word was 'Identical', the clues could not be 'Judwa' or 'Ram-Shyam' or 'Whimsical' but could be 'Twins', 'Photocopy' or 'Same'. There had to be great synchronicity between the partners so that the first one knew exactly what clues to give to lead the other's thought process.

Each team got three attempts before the word passed on to the next one. The points for the word—and this is where Adi's eccentric genius shone—would diminish with every try as the contestants had the benefit of their predecessors' attempts. If the three contestants could not guess the answer, the word would be thrown to the live audience.

The scoreboard and timer were handled by the Warrier brothers, and later Adi roped in his attractive assistant Scherezade Modi to help out with the scoreboard. The background of the set would be anything Doordarshan could spare for the day.

What's the Good Word would only air twice a month, but there was about 20 days of work behind every episode. I would go to Adi's office in Fort, from where he brought out the Parsi periodical *Jam-e-Jamshed*. The office looked as if it had been ravaged by war: I would have to weave through a maze of teetering, piled-up books to reach his desk. Yet he knew exactly where each book was. "There's a method to my madness," he would say.

I would go over once or twice a week and sit there for three or four hours, researching words and terminology. There had to be a good mix of politics, history, music, glamour, science, geography and so on. There was a special shelf for all the words we used on air, with references and citations to their origins and where we got them from, in case a fan challenged their authenticity or meaning later.

Thousands of postcards would arrive at the Doordarshan office in Worli every week and be stored in gunny sacks in a room. I would dig elbow-deep into a sack to grab a handful and assess the letters to choose participants. We aimed for a good mix of ages and gender, and then sifted contestants based on word knowledge, adaptability and quick thinking. There were so many gunny sacks that once in a while, someone would come and remove a few lots to destroy to make room for the new ones.

For each show, there would be a preliminary round with 100 contestants, which would be whittled down to 20 and then 6. This meant a bank of at least 60 new words per episode. There could be no repetition of matter because sometimes we met contestants who had been on the show eight times.

There was no Google then and you had to tap your own mind for ideas and scour foreign magazines for new words or colloquialisms. I would research how terms evolved and find a context to present them to the contestants. So many of those words have stayed with me, for example, 'desquamate'. It's the process of the skin shedding its cells during renewal. The question posed on TV would be something like this: Suppose you are in an airtight box and after a period of time, find a thin layer of dust on everything. Where does it come from?

To keep things interesting, we would run themes: the contestants could be siblings, spouses, parent–offspring, twins or mother–son duos. We also introduced a live element—a dance performance (Astad Deboo came on the show once) or a cookery segment, and the audience would be asked the name of a mudra or cooking technique. Of course, it fell upon me to find these performers and cajole them to come on air for a princely sum of ₹50–60.

Mind you, I only earned about ₹130 per episode, but I didn't mind because the work was so enriching and I loved learning new words.

On stage, I would have to be sensitive to the energy of the contestants and audience, and also enunciate well. I would slip in 'What's the Good Word' at least three times during an episode so that the viewers would know what they were watching.

All operations at Doordarshan were powered by tea and a limp *chivda*—there was no budget for a production team, researcher, make-up, wardrobe or food. I wore my own clothes, favouring small prints and shirts to look professional and accessories that didn't distract. A make-up *dada* would do the base and I did the rest of it myself. The contestants and winners were given coupons to bookstores such as Strand Bookstore as prizes.

Because of *What's the Good Word*'s popularity, I became the Quiz Queen of Bombay and was often invited by clubs such as the CCI and Willingdon, or educational institutions such as the Indian Institute of Technology to hold word games. This meant preparing new material as I couldn't use the words I had used on TV. I would even be requested to bring a few 'words' when invited to a party. Sometimes I would comply or would politely say I was looking forward to a relaxing evening.

Many other opportunities came my way thanks to the show, and this was all because of Adi's undying faith in me. He pulled me into everything else he did because he wanted to look no further for a collaborator. I worked as a narrator and interviewer for short films on DD. Some of them were about interesting personalities, such as the famous car collector Pranlal Bhogilal. We chatted about his collection of vintage luxury cars, how he keeps them running and how he modified each one. Another short film was about a lost *bajubandh* (arm band) from the jewels of the Nizam of Hyderabad.

The then editor-in-chief Khalid Ansari approached me to write a column for *mid-day*. We called it 'Mind Your Language' after a famous TV show of the time, and I would talk about the importance of pronunciation and building a vocabulary, or unravel the etymology or usage of a term.

Editor Fatima Zakaria also requested me to write a column for *The Times of India* and I asked for a spot on the left-hand corner of the back page. We called it 'You're Cornered'. It was a multiple-choice general knowledge quiz with the answer given at the bottom, upside down.

Both columns ran for a couple of years. I was grateful

for the opportunity but didn't enjoy it perhaps because of the lack of live human interaction.

In 1986, I approached the management at Doordarshan saying we needed to update the show. It had been running for nearly 15 years and I suggested an electronic scoreboard, more valuable prizes and an audiovisual element. Doordarshan flatly refused to keep up with the times, so Adi and I were left with no option but to bow out.

What's the Good Word kick-started English TV programming in India and catapulted me onto every TV screen in the country—it was first aired only in Bombay and then became a national programme and went into colour. It came on at 9 pm, two Mondays a month, from 1972 to 1986. Where theatre was limited to its aficionados, concentrated mainly in South Bombay and among the English-speaking populace elsewhere, TV was an emerging modern medium. By the 1980s, it was in every middle-class home and slowly becoming the primary mode of entertainment. Shobhaa De, who wrote a column even back then as Shobha Kilachand, called me the voice that India listened to as it shovelled *curry–chawal* into its mouth!

As the programme approached its 15th birthday, on Doordarshan's behest, I wrote to the *Guinness Book of Records* to check whether I had set a record as the longest-serving presenter for a TV show. They wrote back saying I certainly held the record as a female host, however, they didn't compartmentalize the honour by gender and so it was held by British TV presenter Arthur

Bamber Gascoigne, who hosted *University Challenge* for 25 years.

Many people who meet me even today say their parents would insist they watch the show to improve their vocabulary or learn English. I was once pulled away at security clearance in a Canadian airport. As I fretted, a customs officer came up to me and said, "Are you the same lady who used to come on *What's the Good Word*? I used to watch you while growing up and wanted to meet you! You still look the same!" As recently as in 2018, my maid went to see a doctor and told him where she worked. "Oh!" he remarked, "I grew up watching her on TV."

6

How the Theatre Bug Bit Me, and I Bit It Right Back

BY 1963, I WAS on the radio a few times a week, but still restless and sought more avenues to express myself. It was Adi who sowed the seed of theatre in my mind. "You will make a good actor," he said. "You are happy when you are interacting with people and that translates across any medium." I had seen some of his Gujarati plays and knew that it was not my cup of tea due to the language barrier.

When I saw Arthur Miller's *The Crucible*, performed by Alyque and Pearl Padamsee, I was mesmerized. I realized this was what I wanted to do. I asked my uncle Yaseen Wazirali to introduce me to the Padamsees as he was associated with the Theatre Group that they helmed.

I don't know why I didn't consider doing something else such as designing clothes or teaching. I just thought—I like standing up and being somebody else; I think I am going to be good at it. I had no fear of public speaking and was quite the clown in school, imitating the teachers to make my friends laugh.

Uncle Yaseen was a very social person. Like many of that generation, he was westernized, stylish and extremely well-spoken. He knew people in Bombay's literary circles and chaired meetings at cultural bodies such as the Indo-Western Society.

He took me to meet Alyque and Pearl, the ultimate power couple. At the time, Alyque Padamsee and Ebrahim Alkazi were the big names in theatre. They were part of the Theatre Group, and then there was a breakaway faction called the Theatre Unit. Alyque led the Theatre Group while Alkazi took over the Theatre Unit.

"What makes you think you can act?" asked Alyque, giving me the first taste of his acid tongue.

"A feeling deep within me tells me so," I said naively. Remember, I was only 21.

"We don't just plonk on stage anybody who thinks they can act," he said brusquely. "We make them audition to see if they have potential. Then you start at the bottom, doing all the dirty work backstage."

"That's fine by me," I said.

Even as I was auditioning with three other girls, I knew I would get the part. It required a slight French accent, which was right up my alley; the others were just saying their lines.

I was reading from the play *The Word* by Partap Sharma, the velveteen voice behind all the Doordarshan serials and the news. According to the script, I was supposed to be a schoolgirl. "This is the funniest thing," I thought. "I've got three children and they want me to pretend to be a schoolgirl!" But then, what is acting but becoming someone else?

Sure enough, Alyque said, "Fine, you can do the play,

but before that you've got to learn what a demanding mistress theatre can be. I am doing *Hamlet*..." "What do you want me to do there?" I blurted, thinking he was going to give me a role. "Help Pearl with the costumes," he said.

The production had zero money and the play was on a grand scale—there were over a hundred costumes. The only cheap fabric was jute, which came at a few rupees a yard. Pearl and I would buy metres of it, dye it in basic colours on her terrace in *dekchi*s using dyes that actor Farrokh Mehta would procure for us from a factory he was working in at the time. Then we would go to Mrs. Boyer, (Mrs. B, we called her) in Colaba, because she was the cheapest seamstress we could find. She made basic tunics and we rummaged in our own closets for belts and buckles, or went to Sippy Chawl in Crawford Market to source lace and borders to give the costumes a regal flourish.

The leading man was this wonderful actor called Zul Vellani, whose voice was like liquid gold. But his legs were thinner than mine (though he had a large personality). His physicality didn't go with his voice. His costume was a short coat and tights that made him inconsequential. I decided to put about ten tights on him, one after the other, and finally he looked like Hamlet. Alyque thought the idea was great.

After *Hamlet*, I went to the cast party and saw the fun people had backstage. "This is what I want," it dawned on me. "This is my life."

Finally, I got to play the part I had auditioned for, but

first I had to secure my mother-in-law's permission. We are not a very conservative family, but still, with going on stage and acting with men all the time, Chotu felt it was better I checked with her. She was a quiet person and I was sure that she would not object, but if people were going to come up to her and say, "Oh we saw your daughter-in-law prancing around on stage," I felt she would appreciate having been part of the decision.

Ba simply said: "You do what makes you happy and doesn't make my son unhappy."

So, in 1965, I debuted on stage as a schoolgirl who descends a swinging rope ladder. An avant-garde production, *The Word* was set in a nuclear shelter and took place in the basement of a dental college. The audience sat on empty wooden crates used for transporting tinned food, which came from Chotu's factory in Andheri. Alyque's younger brother Bubbles was in the play as was his then wife Pearl. They provided the romantic lead, and senior actor Manohar Pitale, one of the best of the time, played an old man. We were all characters who take refuge in this shelter.

However, I hadn't practised descending the ladder. I had only imagined it during rehearsals which would be held in people's homes or large spaces. When I tried to come down during the first stage rehearsal, the rope went swinging from side to side like a pendulum while I clung on for dear life. "What am I doing?" I thought to myself, "I have three little babies at home..."

An even more unnerving incident had occurred backstage. As I was waiting to descend, someone who was learning the ropes of theatre as I had and was the head of a bank, tried to feel me up. As you can imagine, it was the most unnerving experience before one went on stage for the first time. "Stop it," I said. "C'mon, it's just a little bit of fun," he said, trying to rustle up my skirt. "You stop it right now, or I'll scream."

Eventually, I did get down that ladder, wearing bloomers to protect my modesty, and the play was a success.

The big critic those days was Mr. Mathews from *The Times of India*. People read him, whether we liked it or not, and if he said the play was worth seeing, you could be sure it was going to be a sell-out. If Mr. Mathews said the play was nothing, only die-hard theatre fans would come to watch. But he gave the play a good review and me an excellent one. A Muslim newspaper also wrote how I was the first Khoja woman, from the smaller Ishna Ashari sect, to be on stage.

Soon I started getting offers from various theatre groups, but it was still a limiting vocation. There were only two or three English groups doing one production at a time, and there would be only a few roles that one could fit into given gender, age and capability.

To be in Anton Chekov's *Three Sisters* in 1967–68, under Nisha D'Cunha's direction, was an honour. She was the head of the English department at St. Xavier's College in Bombay then and cast me as the youngest sister Irena. I got a chance to act with a different group of people which included Usha Katra and Nergish Kawasji.

In the late '70s, I did Tennessee Williams's *A Streetcar Named Desire* which was a turning point in my life.

Dalip Tahil was cast, very accurately, as Stanley Kowalski, a character who was imagined as a big brute of a man with animal magnetism and a powerful presence. We had done some readings of the play with Vijay Crishna, who was a good actor, but he did not fit the bill physically.

One night, after rehearsals, Dalip tried to get a bit too familiar. "Look," I said, "I'm not that kind of a person. I'm very happy with my husband and I don't need this kind of attention." But he kept coming on to me and in the end, I just walked away from the party.

Later he told me that he was practising a scene where Stanley comes on to Blanche. But I didn't know that.

The next morning, I called up Alyque to tell him I couldn't be in the play. *Streetcar* was very emotionally and physically intense with a rape scene. I felt I wouldn't be able to give myself to the role if I was physically uncomfortable with my co-actor. I told Alyque this and he said, "You are the only person I see as Blanche—mood wise, talent wise, physically... everything fits."

"I won't be able to act with Dalip because he has come on too strong and I don't think he will change," I reasoned. "I will speak with him and he will come and apologize," Alyque said. "Just leave it to me."

The next day, Dalip sent me a huge bouquet of roses and apologized earnestly. I relented and we became very good friends after that and remain so till this day.

A few years later, in 1985, when I was shooting for the movie *Trikal* in Goa, my daughter Heena came to visit me. And Dalip generously sent her a whole case of wine!

Streetcar was widely appreciated and also watched by Jennifer Kendal, whose family had inspired me to join the theatre when they performed in my school. Incidentally, our children went to the same school, and Jennifer and I would meet often. The day after she watched the play, I found a bucket of white flowers outside my door with a note saying, 'In awe of your talent'. The flowers in themselves were beautiful of course, but what Jennifer had appreciated was the nuance of a crucial scene in which a Mexican lady is heard pedalling flowers in the background. "Flowers, flowers for the dead," she is heard saying as another thread of Blanche's sanity unravels on stage.

I won the All-India Critics' Association award for best actress in 1981 for *A Streetcar Named Desire*.

I believe it to be a unique distinction as it was the only time the award was given to an English play. It was the norm in those days to choose a vernacular play and Bengali theatre had a wealth of talent. Critics from all over India put in an anonymous ballot for a director, producer, an actor or a play, and the award would go to the one with the highest votes.

I had to go to Calcutta, as it was called then, to accept my award. Uma Vaid, my oldest friend, lived there at the time and she went with me to the function. I am grateful she did because it was a very cold affair. Nobody spoke to me, congratulated me or even asked whether I would like a cup of tea. I heard they were upset that a Bengali actor had not won.

The whole show was conducted in Bengali and the only English words spoken were '*A Streetcar Named Desire*', which was my cue to get up and go on stage to receive the trophy. But I was not too disheartened by the snub. Uma and I went home and celebrated the moment with a drink.

Theatre is not without its unintentional comedy. I remember one incident that happened during *Tughlaq*. Kabir Bedi played the title role in the Girish Karnad play. He worked at Lintas at the time and his boss was Alyque whose boss was Gerson da Cunha. It was just a matter of time before he found himself on stage. Incidentally, Kabir did only three plays and we acted together in two of them. In *Tughlaq*, at 28, I played his stepmother. The script hinted at an incestuous relationship between the two.

Alyque produced and directed the play, and being an adman, he knew the power of imagery. He always opened with a strong scene which set the tone of the play. *Tughlaq* had the most vivid scenes I have ever experienced, in India or abroad.

It started with Kabir standing with his arms outstretched, like a Christ figure, his back to the audience. He wore nothing but a red loincloth—every muscle in his body glistened under the spotlights. Two manservants entered, one from each side of the stage, and slowly cloaked him in layer upon layer of clothing. As he turned around, they put on the final item—a beplumed crown—and we saw the emperor. The scene depicted the vulnerable human being under all the layers of society.

In the wings, human frailty of another kind was on display. I was waiting for my entry in a magnificent bottle green-and-gold Moghul costume. Now, every actor is nervous before she goes on stage. We keep rehearsing our lines, and remembering the stage positions and keep an ear out for cues. I was doing so before one show when Gerson da Cunha, who played the imam, came into the wings, tapped me on the shoulder and said, "Sabi, Sabi... What are my lines?"

"Hell," I said. "I have difficulty remembering my own lines. How do I remember your lines? Go quickly, have a look at your script in the green room."

"Alright," he said, "but what's the name of the play?"

"What?" I said, "You don't know which play you are in? Are you mad? I'll shake you up. It's *Tughlaq*."

However, when he came on stage, he was magnificent.

Tughlaq was also the background for my rather unsavoury interaction with the late dancer Protima Bedi. She and Kabir were married at the time, and Protima was a very forthright, forceful, in-your-face kind of a person. I was just 28, and frankly, I'm a bit timid and nervous around people like that. I would never be the first one to approach them.

In the play, I had an intimate scene with Kabir in which he sat on the floor, took his shirt off and I massaged his shoulders and stroked his hair. It was an important way of alluding to the intimacy between the two characters and the stepmother's lust and love for the emperor. We were rehearsing one day at the theatre, and as per the script, Kabir came in a *lungi* and sat down at my feet, and I began running my hands through his hair.

Protima happened to see this and charged at me screaming, "WHAT DID YOU DO?"

I was baffled, to say the least.

"You touch my husband again and I'll claw your eyes out," she threatened.

I tried telling her that I was a happily married woman with no interest in her husband. "I have three little children at home to take care of," I said. "The last thing I want is to have to do anything with your husband. I don't have the time, nor do I have the inclination."

"But you look like you want to on stage," she said, eyeing me suspiciously.

"That's because the role requires me to show desire," I explained. "I don't desire him as myself... I desire him as the Queen Mother."

"No," she said simply, "that's not going to be allowed."

"Well, you better tell Alyque that," I said, "because he's directed me this way."

So off she marched to Alyque and asked him to cut out that scene. "You don't like it, you don't come to rehearsals, baby," was all Alyque had to say. "I'm the director. I say the scene stays and that's the end of it."

She became very aloof after that.

Kabir was new to Bombay then, and Chotu and I were happy to have him over for parties and dinners. He said it made him feel like he had family in the city. Though I made many overtures to convince Protima that I was a home-loving, husband-loving creature and not a saucy seductress, she never really warmed up to me.

Another hilarious episode happened during Eugène Ionesco's *Exit the King* in Calcutta. Alyque was performing as King Berenger and I played the older queen Marguerite while another actor played the younger queen. We were standing in the middle of the stage at a very crucial moment: The 400-year-old king has depleted and now lies as a vulnerable, shrunken man. He has to accept the eventuality of his death.

In the middle of all this sombreness, the audience starts laughing.

"What did we do wrong?" I thought to myself. I checked my costume and glanced at the stage. The only prop on it was an imposing throne and the *chaiwallah* was sitting on it, with his tin kettle and cups, enjoying the play.

He must have come backstage to collect his money, and since nobody was there, wandered onstage, saw this nice big chair and thought he could finally catch the play!

Getting under the skin of a character is intense; it takes ages to ease oneself out of it. When I was in *Three Sisters*, there was a lot of weeping and crying. I used to come home very morose. Finally, Chotu said, "Listen, you can't bring your theatre life here. You can't come home and be sad about everything."

He was right. It's not fair to your partner to carry your work worries home and I started researching small tricks I could use to switch off.

I learnt that the Japanese have a tradition of leaving

their shoes outside their home to signify leaving their problems at the threshold. I began using music to change gears—peppy music would pull me out of an intense, morose mood. Likewise, seven to eight deep breaths help me get into character and also to snap out of it. This also makes me feel lighter.

It took every exercise I knew to keep myself afloat while I was doing *Duet for One* in the '70s. It was based on the life of the famous cellist Jacqueline du Pré who was struck by multiple sclerosis in the prime of her life and career. Pearl directed it and cast me as the protagonist Stephanie, a celebrated violinist. Vijay Crishna played my psychiatrist. The play follows Stephanie's six sessions with the doctor as she descends into the depths of human tragedy. "I haven't washed my underwear in two weeks," she tells the doctor at one point. "It's beginning to smell. It's a nice smell." In another session, she confides how she has been buying copper tubing to lure the totter into her bed. "He flings me about like a sack," she says, "but at least it's better than nothing."

To play this person who was once the most celebrated musicians in the world, one half of a golden couple with pianist and conductor Daniel Barenboim, and was now confined in a wheelchair with no one to care for, was the most emotionally and creatively satisfying role for me. She turns the tables in the last scene when she says that nothing can replace the violin, but she has given it away and must learn to live without it just as she has to learn to live without her husband and the psychiatrist.

That's when we realize it is the psychiatrist now

dependent on her and their frequent interactions. The last line we hear as the lights fade is him saying hopefully, "So, same time next week?"

This play is the closest to my heart. I would weep and weep while doing it and so would the audience. I remember the governor of Maharashtra, Ali Yavar Jung, came to watch a show and he was in tears too.

At other times, you get so deeply under the character's skin that the feelings persist offstage. For instance, when I was cast as Emilia (Desdemona's maid) in *Othello*, many reviews said I stole the play away from the lead actors because I played it with such sincerity.

I imagined her to be a guttural person who was motherly towards and protective of Desdemona. Apparently, I played Emilia with such conviction that even my co-actors were swept away. The actor Nikhila Moolgaoker, who played Desdemona, grew very close to me and shared a very uncomfortable secret.

She was married to a Maharashtrian gentlemen but fell in love with Kabir Bedi (who played Othello) during the play. "You are the first person I have told because you are so protective towards me in the play. I feel you would be the same way towards me in real life," she said.

You could have knocked me down with a feather. "How could it be?" I asked, "you are married; your husband loves and trusts you."

"What can I do?" she said, "I have fallen in love."

"Listen," I told her, "Kabir has fallen in love with half his leading ladies. He's a very attractive man, and a very sexual person. But you can't just leave your life and go after him. He is not marriage material. You want to have an affair with him, you go have an affair and play it out."

But eventually, they got married and she became Nikki Bedi. So sometimes, there is a play within a play, and if you play your character too well, you have to manage real life too!

People around me often fell in love with their co-stars. I have wondered about why I never gave in to the charms and temptations of other actors. I think this was because I was so much in love with my husband and had so much security at home. Whatever I needed—emotionally or physically—I got from Chotu. I never had to look outside for it. And it's not that people didn't try. There would always be a flirty nudge or an invitation to a drink but I would decline saying, "Sorry, I am not that kind of a person." To give my partner any angst or pain would be absolutely against my nature.

My work was also physically dangerous. I was injured grievously twice—once during a show of Maxwell Anderson's *Winterset* and the other time during a show of *The Interpreters*. There was a pit excavated backstage and a plank placed over it to help people cross it. I misjudged my step and fell into the pit, scraping the entire length of my thigh. My flesh was completely raw and exposed. I would be in agony each time my skirt brushed against it. And I had a show the next day!

During *The Interpreters* in 1987, I rolled over some props backstage and fell down. My colleagues had to bring me back home because I was so bruised and in shock. Then we found that the lift wasn't working so I had to climb all the way to the 10th floor!

Sometimes I did a play twice, with different directors or productions, like *Death of a Salesman* by Arthur Miller. I played Linda Loman 20 years apart—once in the '80s, directed by Pearl Padamsee and once in 2012, with Alyque. Jim Sarbh, who is now making his name in the movies, played one of the Loman sons.

There is a world of difference between the two productions, not just because of the gender of the directors and their styles. What is remarkable about acting is that it is a dynamic profession and the years can change your perception of the role.

In the 1980s, I played Linda; in 2012, I was her. I could sympathize with her because by then my children had given me enough grief over the years, I had had grandchildren and seen a few more vagaries of life.

Similarly, if I had to play Blanche again today, I know my whole approach towards the role would change. I was not sympathetic towards her when I first played her—I was angry with Dalip (as the character), and envious of and angry with my sister (Stella) because I felt that life had given her a better deal than me. But now, I would play her with a lot more empathy.

This is also the reason why this is the right time for me to play a female version of Caesar, though I have done readings of the play for many years with Alyque. It's a role that needs maturity. When you are younger, you think Caesar is just ambitious. You think out of Caesar. Now when I read the part, it is in and as Caesar.

Not all plays are a success. Alyque did one called *Oh Dad, Poor Dad, Mama's Hung You in the Closet and I'm Feeling So Bad* in 1968 or 1970. I played a siren who seduces a young boy, and the play ran for only four shows. Finally, an exasperated Alyque handed us the leftover tickets and said, "Here. Use them as toilet paper."

I have done the largest number of plays with Alyque, and been instrumental in the very few occasions that he broke his cardinal rule—that of no drinking on stage (or backstage). I agree that it's really bad form.

Alyque has allowed people to have a drink during a production only twice in his life. The first time was in 1964, during *Hamlet*. I was doing the costumes and working backstage, and even though it was only my first play, I had already become the go-to girl.

Just before the play began, an actor in his 20s, who played a crucial courtier, developed a case of nerves. "I-I am not going on stage," he said. I ran to get hold of Alyque, who only lashed out. "Give him one tight slap. What does he mean he is not going on stage?"

"Now what do we do about this?" I asked realistically. "Go find out who is carrying alcohol," he said. "I know someone must have a stash." I remembered seeing an actor who played one of the soldiers slipping in a drink, and asked her for her hipflask.

She was quite shocked and asked me if I was sure. She finally relented and Alyque asked me to pour a double shot and make the actor drink it. But he was having none of it: "No no, I am going home." "You jolly well drink this," I said, nearly pouring the drink down his throat. Once he had gulped it, he was full of courage. "I'm happy," he said, impervious to all the anxiety he had caused. "Let's go do the play!"

The second time Alyque allowed anyone to drink was when we were doing *A Streetcar Named Desire* in New Delhi. We were doing two shows a day when the Minister of Information and Broadcasting of the time came up and said he had heard so much about the play that he would like to come and watch it at 9.30 pm.

We didn't have a 9.30 pm show. "We'll create one," said Alyque. The minister would be coming with his entourage anyway, so we advertised the show, and again had a full house.

I don't think there has been a demand for a play to have three shows a day, like a movie, before or ever since. It was an emotionally and physically taxing script, not to mention the upheaval of the rape scene.

And now to have to do that three times in one day!

"I'm so tired," I said to Alyque. "I know, darling," he replied, "but what can I do? I have to demand this of you because it's the Ministry of Information and Broadcasting."

When I was ready to go on stage, he brought me a nice double scotch and said, "This time, I am asking you to have it because you are so exhausted. You need something to boost you. You just take this drink, and knock them dead."

And we did!

Sometime in the early 2000s, we embarked on a great adventure. There was a novel play called *The Rummy*

Game, which I had done with two different actors: under Sam Kerawala's direction once in 1998–99 with Hosi Vasunia as my partner, and then in 2011 with Alyque.

Noted businessman and philanthropist Mahendra Mehta happened to see the version with Hosi, and wondered if we would stage it abroad to raise funds for a charity close to his heart—Project Mainstream, which provides food to about 6,000 street kids daily, to this day.

He had the ambitious idea of taking it to the Gujarati diaspora (the play was in Parsi Gujarati) in London, New York, Europe and Canada as the NRI community is very generous.

We agreed to give him the proceeds from the play and travelled like a struggling production, chipping together for the tickets of the crew members who could not afford to make the trip, staying with friends and performing in venues that were loaned to us at minimal rates, if not for free.

Actor Boman Irani, who was a photographer then, did the pictures for the brochures and all the publicity spots. People just opened their homes to us. The YMCA gave us a great big hall in London. In Antwerp, we placed a translation of the play on the seats. Then a very charitable gentleman invited us to Düsseldorf, and Ashaben, Mahendrabhai's wife, had the idea of distributing *khakra*s during the interval to give the whole experience an even more Indian touch. In Canada, the venue was a college auditorium and I had to iron my costume on a little cushion.

In New York, there was five feet of snow on the roads on opening night and Salman Rushdie was to be our guest of honour.

As it is the Big Apple is hard to slice through and here we were blocked in by the weather and quite sure that not too many people would brave the Arctic conditions. But Salman trudged through stoically, as did many other people, and in the end we had a good gathering.

In Chicago, we performed in the hall belonging to a Jain temple. After the show ended, a gentleman stood up and just pledged some money. Then another one joined and then another. Soon, it became a charity auction and we collected something like $30,000 in one evening!

While we were performing *The Rummy Game* in Antwerp for the large Gujarati diamond trading community settled there, they began caring for me so much that they asked me to train them in soft skills—speech, mannerisms and networking, all the things I was effectively doing through Corporate Finesse.

"How do we grow?" was their big question. So, we organized two-day training workshops for the younger lot and I found myself going back essentially to what I learned while socializing with my father.

The community was not growing, firstly, because they were not meeting anyone besides their own people. The Shahs were going to the Desais, the Desais to the Patels and back to the Shahs. "Are you so important that people will come and talk to you? Then why do you sit in a corner at a party?" I asked them.

I taught them the little niceties to help them expand their social circle, such as making something to eat and taking it over to their neighbours or chatting with them over a cup of tea instead of going to a Patel's or Desai's home.

I also found that they were not socializing at seminars; instead of going to the bar where most of the post-seminar business happened over drinks, they would just go back to their rooms.

The biggest roadblock, it seemed to me, was that they didn't drink and thus did not know how to mingle in the western scenario.

You see, the Jewish people would go out and get the diamond business, while our people would be sitting in the corner, nibbling on vegetarian food and leaving early.

I taught them how to pretend to have a drink—a little apple juice in a champagne flute topped up with soda did the trick. After that, it was just a matter of teaching them how to shake hands and clink glasses!

Little did I know that they could teach me a thing or two about fitting in!

I was once invited over by a family and they asked me what I would have before dinner. "A scotch and soda," I said, which is my evening drink. "Oh," they said, "we don't keep it, as we don't drink alcohol." "Then I'll have a soda and scotch," I retorted, and they began laughing. "C'mon," I said, "I know you must be having some scotch or vodka in the house." "Okay, we'll pull out some, but you mustn't tell anybody," they said, conspiratorially.

As they were pouring my drink, the husband said, "I'll

have a small one too." Another couple joined us later, saw the bottle and said in an accusatory tone, "Oh, you are having a drink, are you?" "This is all my idea," I said apologetically. "I usually have one before dinner." "Well then," they said, "we'll have a peg too!"

Now the ladies were feeling left out. "Why don't you bring out the wine," my host told his wife. Then came the clincher: "Don't tell them we have non-veg in the house," said the wife. She was Muslim and they used to eat meat at home, but abstain outside to fit in.

I learnt that the world is full of surprises and you must just enjoy yourself without thinking of keeping up with the Joneses all the time. Eventually, their business increased so much that they invited me over a second time to hold a similar workshop.

And this time, we all had a drink.

Theatre taught me little things and big things such as split-second timing, how to be self-reliant and organized about my props and costumes. To this day, I carry a little kit containing safety pins, hairpins, a needle and thread and some tape whenever I travel or am doing a play. I have always planned my outfits for the week, but with theatre I learnt to arrange them in the order I put them on, and keep them ready—ironed, with buttons and hems in place—the night before. People are always surprised at how quickly I get dressed.

I have always been an instinctive actor. I am able to think like other people and put myself in their shoes. I ask the director to give me an outline of the role, and when I start reading the play, I create a life for her out of the written word. Like perhaps, she might enjoy a Coke but not potatoes. I imagine what her friends must be like.

I don't like discipline to the extent where there have to be precise steps taken on stage; it's more a midground of freedom within the ambit of the role.

Pearl would always ask me to get into the character's skin before a show, so much so that if someone asks me a question, I would have to answer as that character. I still do that on the day of the show and certainly when I get into costume.

Sometimes, I prepare by observing people. When I played Shirin again in the *The Rummy Game*, I was in my 70s. I would visit old age homes, and went to the Parsee General Hospital to study how senior citizens from the community moved and spoke, their reactions to things, the lilt in their diction, the voice, etc. I wound a bandage tightly around my leg as Shirin to get that slightly hindered step.

I love meeting people because I enjoy noticing their individual characteristics. It's a fun exercise to tune into their frequency and speak their lingo—the phrases, topics of conversation, areas of interest—and become them.

I once went to an acting workshop held at the NCPA but found they were not into spontaneous acting. They said you must speak to your character and so on and that didn't appeal to me, so I just built on my innate ability to empathize with people and see their points of view. I really do think people are fascinating and they have been my greatest teachers in acting.

In hindsight, the most important thing theatre taught me was how to fight moral battles.

There is a lot of camaraderie in the profession—soul-to-soul talks with like-minded people who knew exactly what you were pulsing about. In contrast, I went home to a totally different world. But I learnt to fight physical attraction towards my colleagues and wave off their advances too. You think to yourself: what is important to me in life? Attraction is momentary while marriage is permanent. It is something you made a commitment to and you must honour that.

Above all, Chotu would say that he was so confident about himself that he had no qualms about me straying. And I could never let moments of infatuation steer me away.

To involve Chotu in my world, I would invite the gang home for fun evenings. On his part, Chotu was always there on the first night of a play and I would tell him what the role entailed, especially if intimacy was involved with a co-actor so that there would be no awkward surprises. I even invited him to the rehearsals of the rape scene in *Streetcar*.

He was my rock in the creative world too. He would make me try on the costumes and practise my lines in front of him, or he would be there when I rehearsed with a co-actor.

I also learnt to juggle home and work and make sure I was not missed. I would ensure the servants knew exactly when to feed the children and take them for their baths.

I would be home to tuck them in bed and cuddle them. I would supervise Chotu's dinner and ensure his drinks tray was ready when he came home. Everything he would want me to do would be done beforehand. I would also leave him loving notes around the house. We were both just utter romantics all through our decades together.

Of all the 'jobs' I had, I would say theatre was my true calling. It is the biggest part of my identity and it set the stage for so many other hats I donned. It made me comfortable with entertainment, and it turned into a natural, instinctive bridge to the cultural space that was Studio 29.

I was also an entrepreneur for a short while in the '90s when I ran a chocolate-packing business.

One of my friends, Elizabeth Ali Khan, owned a chocolaterie called Chocolaterie de Mont Blanc in Geneva, and I would go and spend time there every time I visited her in Switzerland. She would do the most wonderful wrappings with curled ribbons and cornets, and I wondered why we didn't have something similar in India—all we had in those days was a flat cardboard box.

When I came back, I rang up my friend Rita Mulchandani. She was good at accounts, which is not my forte. We got together to form Giftique, choosing a brand name that did not just limit us to chocolates.

My networking skills and love for meeting people came into play as I went out to corporates and asked them to give me their festival gifting business. We also prepared engagement and wedding notices with beautifully-wrapped gifts.

We got a box maker to fashion some innovative handmade boxes—cornets and dice-shaped ones—with transparent packing. We experimented with different kinds of paper to see how they would fold, whether they could carry the weight of the chocolates and so on. We gave them catchy names such as the Transparent 12 and Loaded Dice, and priced them just under what one would pay at the Taj, but Giftique had the edge on presentation.

Rita had done this before, so she was very good with the operations, and Mehroo Pinto of Choc Affaires made the chocolates.

For a short while, we had a counter at the ice cream parlour K. Rustoms' off Marine Drive, and then at Thacker's bookstore at Rampart Row where we used to sell tickets for our plays. We would take turns sitting there, and I really enjoyed meeting a variety of people. We ran this for about five years until Rita moved abroad. Then we sold Giftique to someone else.

My career as a speech and diction trainer for the Miss India contestants grew out of what I learnt in theatre, enunciation being the main part of it. If people can't hear what you are saying, it is pointless *what* you say. I gathered a few exercises I would do before going on stage and made them repeat these five times while standing up for better breath control and throw.

I am very aware of stressing on the right consonants to get accurate pronunciation. I then turn away from the audience I am practising before—it was usually Chotu—to check if the person can still hear me. People tend to lip-read when you speak facing them; if they can still understand you when they can't see your lips, you have got the diction right.

'Betty Botter' is one such exercise I follow for enunciation and teach prospective beauty queens. The other is 'Theophilus Thistle, the Successful Thistle Sifter'. It was even featured in the movie *The King's Speech*. I was quite amazed to know it goes back so far, and is still used today. Then there is 'Percy and Polly Playing Parlour Pranks to Pass the Time at the Party on the Patio'.

What many people don't see or realize is that theatre is all organization and preparation. So, in many ways, my lessons in theatre were a continuation of the discipline and organizational skills my dadima at Villa Vazir instilled in me.

You have to be prepared for all eventualities on stage. I am a big list-maker, which made Alyque warm up to me immediately. I use two diaries—a two-year planner in which I pencil in all the big appointments and projects and a smaller daily diary that I carry with me everywhere. The bigger projects (say, a party on New Year's Eve) go into my planner and I break them into smaller tasks (plan clothes, review accessories, confirm attendance) for my daily diary, which I consult every morning.

Actors are very sensitive people and while we like to paint a picture of a temperamental artist, I have found tact and diplomacy to be far more useful while working with a cast, and it doesn't blunt my ability one tiny bit.

You only need to assert yourself if you are unsure and it is always better to address any conflict one-on-one. If I felt the actor would do better to approach his dialogues differently, I would pull him aside and ask for help. "I think I would like to try this scene a bit differently. Would you mind helping me rehearse it?" I would say. Quite often, something better would come out of the both of us working on another train of thought.

There are of course difficult moments of conflict when matters heat up between actors or the director during a rehearsal. This is when my diplomacy antenna perks up and I call for a quick tea break.

Sometimes we work with actors who have an undue sense of importance. Publicly, I always put myself on the side of such a person so that he doesn't feel like we have ganged up against him. I befriend the person and soothe him. It always makes them more cooperative.

In recent times, working on *The Buckingham Secret* has been very interesting and very different, mainly because I am not working with people my age—everyone else is in their 20s. The oldest person must be around 40.

It started when the writer and director (he also plays the butler) Meherzad Patel came home one evening. "I have written this play about the British royal family," he said, "the NCPA has told me point blank that they will not sponsor it unless I cast you as the queen. There is nobody else in Bombay who can have the diction, presence and physicality required to play Queen Elizabeth II."

I said I was very flattered but the script would have to be good enough to entice me. And I could tell by the thickness of it that it was too long. He graciously trusted me with editing out unnecessary dialogues and reworking some of the unwieldy bits.

Two co-stars, Danesh Irani and Danesh Barucha, helped me with the Parsi-isms and accent by writing out the Gujarati words and phrases in English so I could pronounce them in that distinctive way. Danesh, who was only some 20-odd years old, would be transformed by make-up into the nonagenarian Prince Philip. He would shave his facial hair at every show and then one skull cap would arrest his thick hair. On would go another wig to show a receding hairline and latex would be used to give him wrinkles. He would then adopt a stoop and a slur, completely fooling even the people who had known him all his life.

I ended up investing a lot more in the play than just my acting skills. Many of the clothes came from my closet. The production spent most of their budget on the wig, which was the key to the character. It was expensive because it was made of real human hair that could withstand all the heat-styling and had to be brought from England. They didn't have too much money left over for the costumes which had to be fit, literally, for a queen. So, we used my sharp skirt suits, bought in England and the USA, in bright colours as Queen Elizabeth wears.

It was the most physically challenging play with the highest number of costume changes I had ever worked in. A changing room was erected near the stage for me to swiftly slip in and out of clothes. My suits still lie with the costume department. Such is the price of theatre.

For the play's promotional pictures, we needed imposing chairs and I had just the French provincial chairs for the job at home. We were shooting at the NCPA, using the grand staircase as the backdrop. I wore a silver gown with a blue sash, perhaps the only costume from the costume department, and needed to use the ladies' room. I marched to it in my regal splendour, and as I opened the door, a lady fainted at the sight of me while her companion froze in shock. They thought the Queen of England was in the washroom of a Mumbai theatre!

I made a whole new lot of friends in the play and they would include Chotu and me in every outing. I think I was the only non-Parsi in the production. Even the backstage hands were from the community and most of them were followers of Meher Baba, a mystic from Ahmednagar. Before each show they would hold hands and pray in silence, and always included me in the ritual.

We had quite a scare on the opening night. In the final scene, we were supposed to take our positions on the balcony backstage, which would then swivel around to face the audience. The British royal family was supposed to wave from there and the Queen would say, "Nothing like being back at Buckingham Palace."

But on the very first night, the mechanism that swivelled the balcony caught a snag and crashed backstage. Luckily, none of the actors had taken their positions yet, so we just went to the front of the stage and waved, and nobody knew any better.

Three people influenced my life in the public sphere very much, and what they taught me could be valuable to anyone else.

First was Adi Marzban who I worked with for nearly a quarter of a century on TV, radio and theatre. He had a razor-sharp mind and extraordinary powers of perception. Western music was Adi's great passion and he was the force behind the radio show we performed.

He cast me in a series of comedies, one of the funniest of which was the West End production *Move Over*. We also did a lot of readings at places such as the Max Mueller Bhavan, the British Council and the United States Information Service (USIS), which has a lovely little theatre near Churchgate, with the capacity for about a 100 people. In those days, they would just let you have the place for a cultural activity and invite everyone on their list of expats.

Adi was good at spotting latent talent, something I absorbed and nurtured, and put to use in my Miss India days, which were to come.

I know when a person is going to go places, like Priyanka Chopra. She had that presence, radiance, charm, and most importantly, tenacity to better herself.

Pearl Padamsee was a hilarious human being and my best friend. We spoke or met almost every day. She was a tiny, vivacious person, packed with energy and she commanded such authority. We would call her *choti mirchi*, and she would retort, "*Pata hai na, choti mirchi hi sabse teekhee hotee hai.*"

I first met Pearl outside of theatre in 1961. Chotu and I had gone to a bookstore to buy tickets to *The Crucible.*

I was heavily pregnant with Aly and Chotu lost me somewhere between the bookshelves, so he whistled to draw my attention. Pearl marched up to him and asked, "Do you have a dog?" "No! I am looking for my wife," he said. "She must have a name," she chastised him. "Use it then." Later we found that she was selling the tickets for the play.

Pearl taught me to get into the character by thinking as the character. You have to give yourself situations that are not in the play and wonder how the person would react. I was already disciplined, but she taught me to apply it to theatre. I would learn my lines before anyone else so that I could get the mood and the movement freely without being physically stuck to the script.

When Alyque met Dolly [Thakore], Pearl went through a very bleak period of unrest and zero creative output. After that, she directed *The Serpent* and cast me in it. I never felt torn when they divorced because I was so devoted to Pearl. I was very upset with the way Alyque had walked out on her, but what do you do? That's life.

I still miss her very much and keep a picture of her at my bedside.

From Alyque, I learnt to project my voice and my personality, instead of internalizing it. "Think of that last person in that last row who has paid 500 rupees for the seat," he would say. "He must be able to hear you. You are not performing just for the front row."

He also taught me to connect with people and the importance of keeping up relationships. In a sense, it was a continuation of what my father had taught me all those years ago. Influence in life is a very big thing. It is a way of winning people over.

He maintained a monthly diary, jotting down names of people he met, their numbers, what they did and so on. "You never know when you might need their help," he used to say.

What her friends in theatre say about Sabira

GERSON DA CUNHA: Sabi educated herself in the theatre.

Sabira is one of those people who you don't have to meet regularly or frequently to feel close to. Her persona radiates in a very peculiar way, and so it is not at all surprising that the persona finds its natural place on the stage, as a teacher, and as an example.

I didn't act with Sabi in many plays, and yet I feel that I have.

Her uncle, Yaseen Wazirali, was one of the trustees of the Theatre Group and that is how I met his little niece. I found her, as everybody else found her, a very attractive little girl. We got to know each other better and more closely when she got involved in the theatre.

Sabi the actor is above all, intelligence. She has a brain that understands what the character is about, what the play is about, and what the line is about. Those are three very important things in a performance. So that is one group of things.

The other group of things is the ability to take direction. And I have watched her take direction and completely change her voice, because Alyque wanted it that way. So, she is able to internalize and assimilate direction. That is the second important thing.

And she has played a range of characters. An ability to read so many characters means, above all, you must have a decent brain, which she has. And a keen ear that listens to direction.

One doesn't know to what extent Sabi the persona and Sabi the actor have interacted. Now which one helped which Sabi? Did Sabi growing as an individual help Sabi grow as an actor? Or was it the other way around? But who cares? It's not important.

I think Sabi educated herself in the theatre. She could have got a PhD in a university if she had the time and the patience to do it, but a part of her maturation has come from being in and associating with the people of theatre.

One of the very important things in theatre is that you have to say your lines every time as if it's happening for the first time. To create this illusion is a challenge for the actor as it must come across as unrehearsed. Sabi has the ability to project that, night after night.

There is another thing about her. She is a person of extraordinary compassion. She has a feeling for the other, which not everyone has. And that I think nobody can teach you. You have to be that way to begin with. Compassion is not kindness, it is not generosity. It is something else; it is humanity.

The other thing about Sabi is that one always wonders where else she is going from here. That is something that would interest me greatly. While you may say that Sabi has been in the public eye for ages, I feel that she is one of those people who is constantly growing. She flowers. So, you wonder to what she is going to give her gifts next. Because she still has a lot to give.

~

VIJAY CRISHNA: All of us benefited from Sabira's professionalism.

Like many of us in theatre, Sabira and I first met onstage! I believe my first acquaintance with Sabira was way back in the '70s, with Pearl Padamsee in one of the several productions we were jointly in.

The first production from which I have a very clear recollection of her is Pearl's *The Idiot* staged in September 1977. Like many productions of that time, it was very intense, since we didn't have the restriction that exists today of having to cater to the box office.

I had the good fortune to be on stage with Sabira in several productions after that. In fact, she often used to joke that I had played her lover onstage, then her husband, and finally in a later production of *Death of a Salesman*, she actually played my mother!

What I remember down the years, and still today, is her sense of professionalism and the trouble she took to get underneath the skin of any character she played, which all of us benefited from.

We did a two-person play in 1984 called *Duet for One*—a very intense production involving a lady who had lost the use of her limbs, and her psychoanalyst. We played many shows for various audiences, many of whom were differently-abled, and they often used to think that I was a real psychoanalyst, so intense was our interaction.

The previous year, quite amusingly, I had staged a production written by a friend of mine, Kersy Katrak, at Studio 29 run by Sabira. The part that I was playing was that of a waiter and just before the show actually began,

Sabira's son Saleem came up to me and asked me to get him a drink. I fobbed him off, and he angrily went to Sabira and complained! She laughed and told him, "Don't you recognize Vijay?!"

Theatre works in funny ways—one person's sense of purpose quickly makes itself felt and raises the performing levels of everyone! Personally, I think that has been her enormous contribution to her work.

The earliest picture of Sabira's biological family was probably taken in the early '30s: Sabira's father Abdul Hussain and mother Gulshan Thariani with Sabira's brother Saleem and her paternal grandmother.

A portion of Villa Vazir, Sabira's family home, still stands at Bandstand in Bandra. It was designed by her biological father, Abdul Hussain Thariani, for his in-laws.

Sabira's "Mummy" Khatija Vaziralli, née Chittiwala.

Sabira's "Daddy", Hazir 'Haaji' Hussain Vaziralli, during one of his few trips abroad in the '60s.

Sabira, the quintessential Bandra girl dressed in her Sunday best, during a family holiday in Matheran, at 14.

Teenage Sabira with Uma (left), her oldest friend, and another friend in a photo taken in the late 1950s. Uma was Sabira's alibi to meet Chotu when they were courting.

Sabira's and Uma's friendship has endured the test of time. Here they are in 2015.

On the day of Sabira and Chotu's nikkah, February 25, 1960, on the terrace of the bride's Bandra home, Ritland.

A designer from the Philippines requested Sabira to model her creations on board a luxury liner while Sabira and Chotu were on their honeymoon.

Sabira and Chotu dancing. Chotu loved to jive and nudged Sabira to take ballroom dancing lessons after they got married.

Sabira's father Haaji Hussain Vaziralli with her firstborn Aly and her brother Inayat (Nanoo), who was born soon after she was adopted.

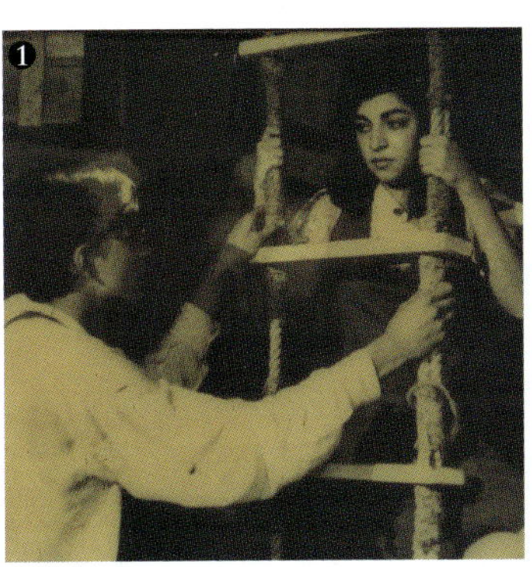

❶ Sabira debuted on stage in Partap Sharma's *The Word* as a schoolgirl, though she was 21 and a mother of three at that time. The play was directed by Alyque Padamsee.

❷ The iconic rape scene from *A Streetcar Named Desire*, in which Stanley Kowalski (Dalip Tahil) takes Blanche DuBois (Sabira) to his bed. The play drew many accolades and Sabira won the All India Critics Association Award for best actress in 1981 for her performance.

Sabira was a popular game show host in the '70s and '80s. Seen here as a contestant on the special episode of another game show with now movie producer Ronnie Screwvala and actor Jayant Kriplani.

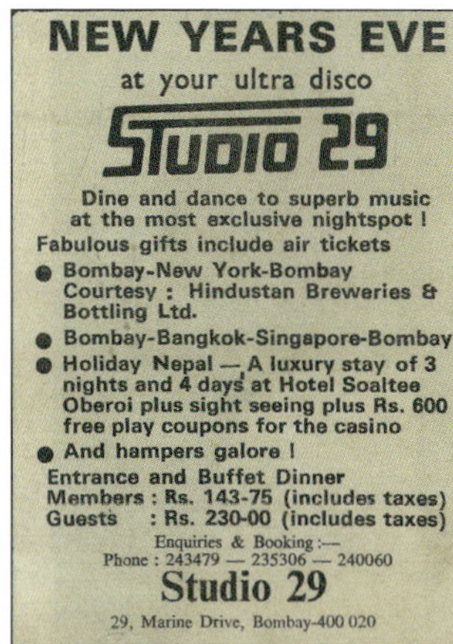

Sabira designed the logo for Studio 29 herself. The place became a favourite hangout spot of the who's who of Mumbai in the '80s and '90s.

Sabira in Shyam Benegal's movie *Trikal* (1985) as a Goan-Portuguese matriarch settled in Lisbon.

Sabira and Chotu dancing at their daughter Heena's wedding reception in 1984 at the Plaza Hotel in New York City.

Sabira and Chotu celebrating their 25th wedding anniversary at the Taj Mahal Palace in Colaba in 1985. Chotu's brother Mammu, his wife Neelu (in a sari) and Sabira's friend Laila Sippy seen in the picture with the couple.

The poster of the play *Deceptions* (1988) showing Sabira and Naseeruddin Shah. This is Sabira's only play with the illustrious actor.

Pearl Padamsee on her 60th birthday in 1990. Sabira's career in theatre started with doing costumes with Pearl. They stayed best of friends until Pearl passed away in 2000.

With actor-filmmaker Dev Anand, who toyed with the idea of making a movie about a beauty queen and approached Sabira to play a herself in it.

In front of the portrait by famed British photographer Desmond Groves, who has clicked many cherished images of Queen Elizabeth II and the British royal family.

Shirley Mataxis, Sabira's roommate when she was at La Chatelaine in Saint-Blaise, Switzerland and the only person she spoke to in English during her time there, with her husband.

Sabira and Chotu with all their grandchildren at a family wedding in 1999. From left: Zarvaan, Azhaan, Kabeer, Karina, Armaan and Arjun.

With Farid Currim and Vijay Crishna in *Betrayal*, Pearl Padamsee's last play.

Chotu with the flamboyant Wajid Ali Khan in 1999.

With Wajid Aly Khan's former wife Elizabeth in 2000. She inspired Sabira to start her packaging business, Giftique.

With Miss World 1999 Yukta Mookhey whom Sabira coached for the contest. Photo taken in 2000.

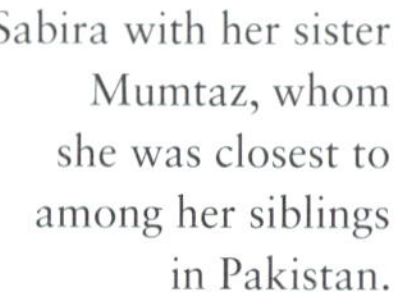

Sabira with her sister Mumtaz, whom she was closest to among her siblings in Pakistan.

The promotional photo of the play *Rummy Game* with Sabira and Hosi Vasunia in lead roles was taken by none other than Boman Irani, who was a photographer before he became an actor.

With Sabira's "BFF" Jimi, her husband Ranjan who was the head of O&M and Chotu—a cozy, close-knit group.

Sabira's brother Inayat (Nanoo).

Monica Vaziralli, celebrated as one of Mumbai's most elegant people, is Sabira's sister-in-law (wife of her brother Inayat) and a close friend.

With Miss Universe 2000 Lara Dutta, whom Sabira coached for the Miss India pageant.

With Raëll Padamsee (centre), Pearl Padamsee's daughter, who calls Sabira her second mother, and Bakul Patel (right), another close friend.

Just after Aishwarya Rai and Sushmita Sen won their respective crowns in 1994, Pradeep Guha of The Times Group approached Sabira to help groom the Femina Miss India contestants for the global platform. Seen here with some of the Miss India aspirants.

Sabira's eldest brother Saleem and his wife Shamim. Sabira's younger son is named after this brother.

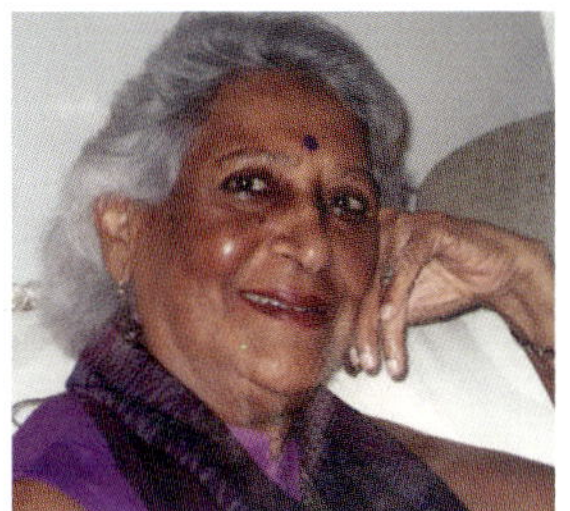

Malu Divecha was Sabira's close friend and gallery-hopping companion.

Sabira with her daughter Heena, who has grown into her soulmate.

With some of the staff at Taj Mahal Palace as part of Corporate Finesse project in 2014.

Chotu and the Merchants' close friend, Charlotte, deep in conversation. For 20 years, the Merchants enjoyed Charlotte's hospitality at her fourteenth-century home in Switzerland whenever they visited the country.

With Jim Sarbh, Neel Tolani and Alyque Padamsee in the play *The Death of a Salesman* (2014).

Sabira and Katayun Engineer (nee Baxter) [third from left, back row] were school friends. Co-incidentally, their children Tayunaz (in red) and Saleem married each other. Seen here with Cyrus Engineer (in violet) on Chotu's 80th birthday.

With Alyque Padamsee (right) and Gerson da Cunha (left) during a rehearsal for a Shakespeare reading in 2017.

Saleem became Sabira's strength and shield after Chotu's passing.

Sabira and daughter-in-law Tayunaz share a loving bond.

Sabira in the musical *My Fair Lady* produced by Rael Padamsee's ACE Production in 2019.

In a rare moment, all of the Merchant grandsons came together in NYC in 2019 — Arjun Pai, Zarvaan Merchant, Armaan Pai and Azhaan Merchant.

In September 2019, just before the world was shut down by the Covid-19 pandemic, Arjun Pai married Annie Rosen in New York. He is the first of Sabira's grandchildren to get married.

Arjun's wedding also brought together the extended Merchant family. Seen here: Parents of the groom, Dhananjay and Heena Pai (far left and to Sabira's right) with Chotu's niece Natasha Merchant (between Heena and Sabira) and her husband Rohit Pappu (second from left), Tayunaz and Saleem, and sister-in-law Monica Vaziralli. Old friend Laila Sippy (between Sabira and Saleem) and Yasmin Sayed (Sabira's left), daughter of Pearl Sayed—London guardian to the Merchant boys—also attended.

7

How I Helped Disco Fever Take Over Bombay

STUDIO 29 CAME OUT of a chance meeting of two strangers at a hair salon on a rainy afternoon. It was nothing less than sleight of hand by fate.

It was 1978 and I was at Patsy Leon's in Tardeo. While I got my hair done, it rained so much that the streets were flooded and the water was waist-high. My dinky car was all but submerged. A wonderful Parsi lady, Daisy Vazifdar, who was also at the salon, offered me a ride in her SUV and we waited the downpour out at her Warden Road home. As we nibbled on *akuri* and toast, her husband made me the most extraordinary offer: "There is this hotel on Marine Drive, which is going to be leased," said Jehangir. "We can't bid for it because it belongs to an Islamic trust, and can only be leased to Muslims. Do you think you would like to go into business with me?"

Jehangir was certainly not in the habit of making business partners out of people he had just met, but he knew of me through TV and theatre, and was a highly astute businessman. He knew my reputation combined with my last name would win the members of the Islamic trust over.

I went home to discuss this with Chotu who had his reservations. He had never run a hotel before, and while I was ready to bulldoze ahead with my creative ideas for a sweet little hotel, he was concerned about the business side of it.

"You don't worry about the daily running of the place," reassured Jehangir, whose family owned Heritage Hotel in Byculla. He was a self-made man: an architect and a recognized artist, and like my late father-in-law Kaka-ji, an instinctive businessman. He didn't live with his head in the clouds like so many creative people.

He and Chotu discussed things and eventually my husband got excited about trying his hand at something new. We became one of the first working couples of the day. It was not common for women to go to business meetings in those days, and just like my father so many years ago, Chotu realized what an asset I could be. When you bring your wife to a loan sanction meeting, it gives you an air of solidity. People see a couple who are working to better their lives and a family man always seems trustworthy.

We found it as easy to work together in business as we had in a romantic partnership. The key was to learn to compartmentalize and trust each other with the assigned roles. I would never interfere in the money aspect and he would leave me to my artistic devices.

While Jehangir and Chotu handled the business side, Jehangir's son Phiroze, an architect, was with me to oversee the day-to-day running of the place. Phiroze is now a restauranteur in London and many cities in India, and the man behind Royal China, Jia and Kuai Kitchen in Mumbai.

The hotel, originally christened Dar-ul-Habib, was then called the Bombay International; it stands today as the Marine Plaza. And to tie up this gift from fate, we found that the building was designed by Bapaji, my biological father, as a hotel for those heading to or coming from Haj. He had even waived off his professional fees in service of the community.

The main clientele was Arabs who were drawn to the view of the sea and the glamour of living on the Queen's Necklace in this pulsating city. We had a charming employee stationed at the airport who would entice the foreigners to check out our rooms (there were no Internet bookings, of course).

To keep the hotel looking fresh, we needed to touch up the paint often, and the man to go to for that was Farokh Messman, now better known as the father of Kainaz Messman (of Theobroma fame).

The business was doing well but I felt the place was not reaching its potential.

Around this time, *Life* magazine came out with an arresting cover: a woman in skin-tight, shiny pants dancing away under a headline that announced 'Disco takes over'.

That grabbed my attention. 'Disco', the truncated version of 'Discotheque', formed an essential part of the zeitgeist of the period. Shiny clothes and accessories, dance music, a nightclub and the dance form—they were all 'Disco'. But the discotheque at the Taj was decaying and the one at the Oberoi was getting weary too. Outside of five-star hotels, the only option was a seedy place where men went to get drunk. Bombay International was perfectly placed to host a high-class sort of place.

There was one hitch though: the only area it would fit into was the rounded corner on the ground floor. It needed to be a buzzing place that people could walk in and out of, and not have to use an elevator. But that would displace a very popular barber's shop called The Wanderers. All of Marine Drive came to it and we weren't sure whether Jehangir would like the idea of moving it. So, I was given the task of tackling him. I showed him the magazine and said, "Jehangir, let's have a discotheque where the barber shop is. What do you think?" "But where will the band sit?" he asked me, incredulously. The idea of music coming through a machine instead of live musicians was still to catch on.

The solution was to raise The Wanderers to the first floor, in place of a few rooms which meant loss of revenue. But Jehangir was able to see our point that an accessible nightclub would easily make up for that loss and more.

So, we gave The Wanderers a new lease of life: plush white leather chairs, spotless white uniforms for the staff, a ceiling-to-floor wallpaper depicting a palm tree-lined sea shore, and moved it to the first floor. I also taught the staff soft skills such as how to greet the customers, make small talk while servicing them and how to remember their names.

There was one more hurdle: the place was owned by an Islamic Trust and drinking is taboo within the religion.

It was left to me to bell the cat: I met the trustees and told them about our idea for a nightclub. "And of course such places have to serve alcohol," I slipped in, "we will not make any money otherwise." They had their reservations, but they were not completely against it because they knew us as family people and were aware of my biological father's piety.

Initially, we thought we would work on a tight budget: a local music system and a Catholic boy from Bandra as the DJ. I envisioned a very 'Dum Maro Dum' feel with straw mats on the floor, but with a touch of class.

Of course, that's not how it turned out!

My years on stage and in studios had taught me the importance of sound. I could not settle for substandard equipment, and since we were in the hotel business and had the license to import, we decided our 'one' big spend would be a top-notch sound system. But then we would need a sound engineer to design the acoustics so that the music and beats didn't bounce about.

Now where does one find a sound engineer in India in the late '70s? I asked around in my theatre group and up popped the name 'Mick Jones of London'. He was renowned as a complete wizard because he knew all about sound, acoustics and light—everything that made a disco a success.

So, we made a trip to London to visit the dance clubs he had designed and found them to be right up our alley. Finding the right 'Mick Jones' in the telephone directory was a herculean task; instead we went about asking the management of the nightclubs for his number. However, sensing competition, they would hesitate to give it to us. Finally, we showed them our passports to prove we were Indian and could not start a business in London. "We're going to start one in Bombay, India," we reassured them.

They grudgingly relented and we were able to meet Mick, a tiny, unassuming person, who took us around to choose things for the discotheque.

A small round table was one of the first things I fell in love with. It had a spot in the centre for a candle for intimate lighting, with a cavity to drop off cigarettes (yes, you could smoke indoors those days) which travelled through the pole to the bottom. In the morning, you would screw off the bottom and clear out all the cigarette butts.

We picked out a few more things for our new venture, and then brought Mick and his wife Lorna to India and put them up at the Bombay International. He sat with an architect-cum-interior designer and drew out the table I had fallen in love with as well as other details for our discotheque and slowly the bills started mounting. We began getting nervous since this was also Jehangir's money. He was after all the majority stakeholder in the enterprise. I really prayed my gamble would work out because it wasn't popular yet to spend the evening dancing to a black record.

First came a mirrored ball, of course, and Tivoli lights on the floor that would dance to a dizzying effect. Then came a machine that would rain bubbles on the dancers.

We initially started with strobe lamps, but eventually had every possible kind of light and the place looked like something out of the movie *2001: A Space Odyssey*. We told Mick that the music had to be way out there too, and he designed a futuristic sound with music from the genius Greek composer Vangelis.

That is how the nightly light-and-sound show was conceived. First the lights would come on, one by one. Then the colour strobes would throb. As the crescendo built up, bubbles would cascade down, the mirrored ball would swirl and lightning would streak on a pillar. Then every element would come alive at once and it was pure fantasy. Onlookers called it a piece of heaven and its fame drew to the Studio both the Showman himself and a noted don.

The inside of the discotheque was split into two—there was a bar side with deep pink plush sofas, and there was the dance floor. They were separated by a one-way mirror so that the people at the bar could watch the dancers, but dancers could not see them, and it insulated the sitting area from the music. The wall on the bar side was tiled with black and silver portraits of Marilyn Monroe, because I was obsessed with her. Her face was also on the mugs and T-shirts, along with the disco's logo, that we gave members.

We served finger food at the bar, a signature drink and a bowl of milk for model Aarti Gupta's little Lhasa Apso, Dumpling, who always accompanied her and was a legitimate card-carrying member of Studio 29.

A sacred place was carved out for the disc console and the jockey, since it was such high-tech and expensive equipment. Nobody was allowed to go there, not even Chotu and I. We covered the walls in grey flecked carpets to absorb the sound, and the end effect was really so divine that no matter how loud the music was it didn't bounce about, but hit you right in the sternum.

When the time came to give it a name, we wanted something that would not restrict its purpose. There was a Studio 54 in New York City, inspired by which we went with Studio 29, the number denoting its plot number on the iconic Marine Drive.

Now it needed a logo, so I went to my theatre friends who were in advertising, but agencies demanded a minimum investment of one lakh rupees! By then we had run out of money, so I thought I would jolly well design it myself. After all, I had taken art lessons in Saint-Blaise.

It had to be something racy, so I extended the 'S' and played around with 29. Then we went to the newspapers and had them print it out for us. I also designed the uniform for the staff—Wilma Saldanha and Shirin Manekia, who sat at the front desk, wore black-and-silver tops with a black scarf lined with silver and the logo etched on one end. Chotu's first cousin and Shirin's husband, Mohsin Manekia, a man of finely-tuned diplomacy, oversaw the entire space as the manager. A boxer called Brian Sopher was stationed as the bouncer and Elias Pereira served as the F&B manager. And thus, it became a family-run place.

Tempers would fly often, but Mohsin knew how to diffuse the situation. "Oh, come on brother, let's go have a smoke," he would interject, and pull the aggressor away. He was careful to not let things escalate into a fight or get into the newspapers, which spells death for anyone in the hospitality business.

We had decided to keep it an exclusive members-only establishment and through word-of-mouth 30 to 40 people had signed on by the time we were ready. To open strong, we flew down from London a disc jockey, Tony, whom Mick recommended. Pearl Padamsee and Behram 'Busybee' Contractor inaugurated it together on April 29, 1979. We invited an eclectic mix of people—artists, the city's business elite, the haut monde, theatre actors and the Richie Riches. Across from the Studio, on the tetrapods that line the beach, I had a structure built without telling anyone or taking permission from the concerned authorities. This is very unlike me because I am, by nature, a rule-follower. But I knew if I went about asking for permission (I didn't even know who to go to), there was a fair chance that it would be refused. Today, I'm shocked by my audacity! It had the disco's name spelt out in fireworks, and the moment the light-and-sound show ended inside, they went off and Studio 29 blazed across the board.

Phiroze tells me that on the opening night around 300 people were trying to get in. It got really crowded, so he and Mick stepped out to look at the other nightspots in the neighbourhood. They went to the Cellar at the Oberoi, and found hardly 10 people there. They chatted with the staffer at the front desk who told them to go to the newly opened place down the road if they wanted to have a good time!

Chotu was not happy with the disc jockey from London and decided to fire him on the first night itself. Until we found a replacement, Phiroze and some other local lads were in charge of the music. Since the disco scene was nascent and our equipment new, the DJs were more interested in playing the music they wanted to hear rather than what set the crowd grooving. Often, Phiroze would walk into the Studio at 11–11.30 pm and find it packed but with no one on the dance floor. The DJs would make excuses like, "the crowd is just not in the mood today." "They wouldn't have come to a disco if they were not in the mood," he would tell them. An idea struck him: he made a list of 10 'magic numbers'—like 'Funkytown'—that always got feet tapping. Eventually, Chait Karmakar and Joe became our regular DJs.

Within about nine months of opening, we had 700 members and couldn't absorb any more. All the investment came back and Jehangir was very happy. True to his tribe, our Parsi partner was a person of integrity and generosity. We were 40-percent holders, but one day he called us into his office and said, "You've worked so hard, I want to make you a 50-percent partner, and no you don't have to put down any more money." All his friends had told him that Studio 29 was the best thing they have ever seen: "Better than London!" they told him in their lovable Parsi intonation.

Slowly, the Studio took on an artistic life of its own beyond our vision. Since it was unused in the day, and had all the technical equipment needed for performative arts, it became a space for readings, plays, dance recitals and even art display, not to mention, a location for movie shoots.

I knew of a short film titled *The Indian Experience* which was made primarily to give foreign tourists a glimpse of the country. It was a rich audiovisual treat presented across a series of screens that fired up one after the other to create an immersive experience of the country's hustle and bustle. The film usually played in small preview theatres and was perfect for the Studio given the equipment and ambience. So, we procured the permission to play it and slipped pamphlets announcing the show timings under the doors of the rooms in our hotel and those of other five-stars in the neighbourhood.

If I read in the papers that a famous singer or band was in town, I would find a way to approach them and get them to perform at the club. This is how we hosted the iconic disco band Boney M.

Choreographers Shanti and Sangeeta Chopra would present avant-garde fashion shows that were more of performative art set to modern music. Instead of designers, these shows were meant to present the latest fabrics by mills, so the clothes would be outrageously creative and not necessarily about what could be practically worn. After the show, models Anna Bredemeyer, Aarti Gupta and Gazala Chinwalla would change their clothes and hit the dance floor. Eventually, I began picking up 'disco' clothes—tight shiny pants and tube tops from the US and UK for them to wear—and set up a closet at the Studio.

We even hosted some plays. One of them was *The Nightbirds*, which I produced. It was written by adman Kersy Katrak, directed by Pearl Padamsee and set in the basement of a hotel. So, Studio 29 was the perfect location. It starred Vijay Crishna as a waiter, and instead of making an entry on stage, I suggested he pretend to be one of the staff members at the Studio and dust a table or serve a drink and then take up his lines. He was so convincing that my son Saleem asked him to get him a drink!

Stalwarts such as Astad Deboo and Farida Peddar performed there too. My cronies from theatre, like Alyque, would drop by after work and sit in the bar area to talk politics or music and observe the youth.

It became almost a daily hang-out for everyone working on ad filmmaker Kailash Surendranath's set, his wife Aarti tells me. She was Aarti Gupta then, the omnipresent Sunsilk model, and after the day's work, all of them would pile into Kailash's van and head on over to meet their friends. Since she didn't drink alcohol, Elias would serve her a glass of milk.

Cheekily, the superstar Salman Khan reminded me at an event that he would sneak into Studio 29. "I still owe her money!" he said at a public gathering in the 2000s referring to the guest fee. It must have been when he was a model shooting with Kailash.

Aarti also served as the rare bridge between South Bombay and the film folk. When Feroz Khan was researching for his movie *Janbaaz*, he wanted to see a discotheque, and Aarti brought him over. Hema Malini and Dharmendra also shot a song there. One evening, the Showman himself, Raj Kapoor, requested a peek of the light-and-sound show. He came in after we had closed for the night and was gracious and well-spoken. He insisted on sitting on the floor so that he could feel the essence of the place.

Not all our guests were so glamorous. Once, as I was closing up close to midnight, five people on motorbikes came in really fast and almost swung into the Studio. They had scarves around their necks and wore their shirts unbuttoned to the navel. Multiple knife scars were visible on their bare chests; you could tell that these were real hard elements.

Their leader was a don from Malad. He controlled a wide illegal web of alcohol, drugs and other contraband substances. Anything dubious in that area would have to go through him. And he asked for me.

One of the bouncers was with us, as was our British friend, Buddy Newton, who used be a boxer when he was younger. "I'll help you if they want to come in," Buddy said. "No one can help anyone," I said. "We don't want a fight. He knows of me; let's just ask him what he wants."

So, I went up to him and politely asked how I could help him. "*Humko* Studio *mein aaneka hai* (We want to come inside)," he said. "*Humko dekhne ka hai kya hai yeh cheez. Suna hai* Studio 29 *bahut badee cheez hai...* (We want to see what all the fuss is about. We've heard great things about Studio 29)." All I could say was, "*Aayiye... zaroor aayiye* (Please come in)."

He was just so taken aback. "*Aap sab log aayiye* (All of you please come in)," I insisted. "*Aap drinks lenge*? Hard drinks, *ke* soft drink? *Aap hamara* sound show *dekho* (Would you like something to drink? Hard drinks or soft drinks? Come and watch our sound show)."

One or two guests who were lingering in the corner scuttled away. Fortunately, the DJ was there and he quickly fired up the system.

"This is it," I said after it was over, "this is what you've heard about." "*Jannat ke jaisi hai* (It's a piece of heaven)," the '*bhai*' said. Then it was time for my jaw to drop: "*Aaj se toh aap meri behen ho gayee*," he said. "*Aapko kuch* protection *chahiye, toh main yahan pe hu. Aapko koi* bother *kare toh aap kehena ke yeh mere bhai hai*. (From today, you are my sister. If anyone bothers you, you tell them you are my sister)."

Seeing that I was about to leave anyway, he said he would drop me home. "*Do* motorcycle *aage jayegi*, *teen peeche rahegi. Aap beech mein chalana*. (Two motorcycles will ride in the front, three at the back. You drive in the middle)."

"Okay," I said. "My car is parked outside. Do you know where I live?"

"*Mein aap ke baare mein joh jaanna hai, woh sab jaanta hu. Aaap ek sacche dil ki aurat ho* (I know everything about you that is to be known. I know you're a goodhearted woman)," he said. So that night, Chotu and I travelled in a cavalcade all the way home!

But that was only one instance. We were able to keep the disco clean of any kind of drugs or illegal substances. I think it helped that people saw a wholesome couple at the wheel. Our son Saleem, who was back in India by then, would drop in with his friends often. "We were able to have a good night out within just 100 bucks," he would say. “It was enough for cab fare, cigarettes and a beer. Plus, our friends’ parents would easily give us permission to stay out late, since we would be in a place run by my mum and dad.” There was even a man who came every single night for a whole year and we gave him a cup to celebrate his 100 percent attendance!

We kept infusing the Studio with fresh ideas. As ‘disco dancing’ spread, we brought out Studio 29 on Wheels—a white van with the Studio 29 logo painted on it would travel with lights, music equipment, a disco ball and a DJ to whoever wanted to host a party at home or within a smaller space.

Then on one trip to London, we came across shawarmas and it brought to mind the empty conference room on the ground floor at the Bombay International. It was on the other corner of the hotel and had a service window. We put up a grill so one could motor up to the window, pick up a shawarma and a cold drink, and be on their way. We called it the Chuck Wagon, and Usha Khanna, who ran Samovar, also became a part of it. I roped her in to make some utterly delicious pre-packaged meals in bamboo or cane plates—small *dahi vada*s, kebabs, rotis and other bites—that could feed two or three people and be picked up from the Chuck Wagon.

Those years were the busiest of my professional life. My children had all grown up, but I was not yet in my 40s. I became the liaising person for the Bombay International since Chotu and Jehangir were busy handling the numbers and labour. I learned that negotiations are better done in person and to never put on airs. If the income tax officers invited me saying, "You must come and say hello to us...," I would never decline. We would chit-chat about their families over a glass of soda water. I could see how happy it made them that a known personality had come down for a meeting. I even got a certificate called 'Sanman' which was awarded to conscientious high-income taxpayers.

My creative world was densely packed too. Although I saw Adi Marzban about once a week for *What's the Good Word*, I worked on it through the week. In the afternoons and evenings there were theatre rehearsals and shows. And then I would head to the Studio.

One society-watcher accurately captured it in her column, saying, "I don't know how Sabira does it. I watch her go to pieces on stage as Blanche, and then she's dancing the night away on the dance floor!"

A few years into running the hotel, labour trade unions all over Bombay began bristling with discontent. We were affected too. Two of the Bombay International's staff members, Achootan and Vinayak, galvanized a union of the staff members and began demanding more money. We raised their pay but they were not satisfied and threatened to go on strike.

The men were in charge of labour, and Jehangir came up with a very clever idea. He put up a hoarding outside the hotel which said, 'The highest paid staff in the whole of India stays here'. And it was true.

Then one night, as I was leaving the Studio, all of them lay down on the floor, blocking my way. "Why are you doing this?" I said. "I have been very nice, honest and kind to you. You are making a lot in tips and we keep giving you opportunities to grow. You are on the world map. Don't embarrass me like this. We cannot afford to pay you more than this..."

They honoured me. "Madam, you please go," they said. "You are not involved in this." But we continued to have trouble. I had read somewhere that discotheques don't last for more than three years as people tire of the same thing. Studio 29 was already past that date.

When we sensed keen buyers with a serious offer, I saw an opportunity to get out before it was too late. "I cannot run something which I am afraid will shut down at any moment," I told Jehangir. "It could happen in the middle of a show or performance. Plus, I think its lifespan is over. It'll roll downhill if we don't overhaul it completely—change the decor, the concept even. And if we do that, the labour union will think we have the money and give us eternal trouble."

Jehangir agreed and we sold the whole hotel to a family called the Majithias. They had one condition though: To keep the lifeblood flowing, they insisted that I stay on for at least a year after the sale. I agreed and the first thing I told them was to not go or allow anyone to go near the DJ's console. I continued to infuse creativity into the place but it died down a few months after I left.

This disappointed so many of the regulars. Alyque had seen the potential for it to become a refreshing modern art and culture space.

But I think we got out at the right time. It remains a sparkling jewel in people's memory and not a decomposing place that was browning at the edges.

8

A Brush with Cinema

I DID A SHORT stint in the movies, a medium I found dissatisfying because it is not as honest as the theatre. There are great breaks while a shot is being set, and the actor says the dialogue repeatedly, for takes and retakes, which are not shot in a linear fashion. Everything in theatre flows so naturally. You become the role and emote as the character through the duration of the play.

Regarding movies, I have to agree with my friend Alyque who liked to say, "You behave, and then they photograph you."

Nonetheless, I acted in a TV presentation called *Sone Ka Pinjra*, released in 1986. I played a Parsi lady who lives in a simple apartment with her sister and is completely infatuated with the star Sanjay Dutt. There is a scene where the star comes to a party and she starts singing a ditty that went something like "*Dekh ke* Sanjay Dutt *ko pagal hona mangta*." I was really taken aback by Dutt's presence. He was a tall, broad-shouldered man with an imposing presence of virility.

We shot mostly in *chawl*s, and I'll never forget the

kindness of one person. It was a hot day and I must have wilted while waiting for the shot to be set up. A sweet lady in a nine-yard sari with *mangalsutra* and with flowers in her hair beckoned me into her home. "I am just about to sit down for lunch," she said in Marathi. "Have a quick bite with me." She served me a little of the simple food she had made—*sabzi*, *dal* and *phulka*s.

Thus the parting lines from *Streetcar* keep coming back to me: "I have always relied on the kindness of strangers..."

In 1985, I got an opportunity to work with Shyam Benegal in *Trikal*. I had known Shyam when he used to do make-up for our plays. For *Trikal* we lived for a month or more in Goa, shooting in cartoonist Mario Miranda's ancestral home in Loutolim. I played a Portuguese woman who comes to Goa to get her son, played by singer-musician Lucky Ali, married to a local girl. My co-stars were Naseeruddin Shah, Dalip Tahil, Keith Stevenson, Soni Razdan, Neena Gupta and of course, the legendary Leela Naidu, who played the lead.

Leela still had a porcelain complexion, but I will never forget the fights between her and littérateur Dom Moraes. The whole hotel would literally shake as plates were smashed. It was terrifying.

Through *Trikal* I got an opportunity to see how the world of feature films works. To create a foggy atmosphere, a man called Qassim Dhuawala would be summoned. He carried a little *sigri* with red hot coals sprinkled with frankincense, which he would fan to create smoke. To show the passing of years, the house would be painted overnight and whole fields would be replanted with paddy brought from other parts of the state to indicate change of season. It is incredible how hard the people off the screen work, and here I was thinking cinema is contrived acting.

I was away from my family for a really long time while shooting for *Trikal* and our 25th wedding anniversary was around the corner. We were a little tight financially but still wanted to celebrate our life together for a quarter of a century! It's funny now that we thought 25 years was a big deal; altogether, Chotu and I were partners for 56 years!

I coordinated the party from Goa and invited some of the cast and crew. It was held at the poolside in the Taj Mahal Palace Hotel in Colaba. The diamond-and-ruby necklace Chotu had got me needed a spectacular outfit. I entrusted my friend Laila Sippy, who lived in London, to bring me a number. She must have gone to Harrods to procure the pearly white gown with black ruffled off-shoulder sleeves. The soap opera *Dynasty* was all the rage then and everyone said I looked like Joan Collins.

Laila also brought down a framed portrait of me shot by Desmond Groves who has photographed Queen Elizabeth of England and her family. On a trip to London the year before, we found that Groves had set up a studio at Harrods and was open to commissions. Chotu and I went to get our portraits shot. I was wearing a white, pleated one-shouldered dress and Groves put me in the foreground of a Persian carpet. He was so pleased with the outcome that he displayed a blown-up version of the picture next to a portrait of King Hussein of Jordan at his studio. So, most people presumed I was one of the king's wives!

I also played Madame Maneckshaw in a BBC production titled *Sixth Happiness*. There was a personal connection to the film. The writer Firdaus Kanga's mother, Tehmi, was my father's secretary for a very long time and remembered me coming to the office as a child. Firdaus had seen my favourite play *Duet for One* in which I was in a wheelchair. He decided I was perfect to play his mentor Madame Maneckshaw and insisted I be cast in the movie. The script was based on his autobiography *Trying to Grow*.

Kanga was born with the brittle bones disease and would literally break a rib every time he hiccupped. Mine was a small but effective role: Madame Maneckshaw was his mentor and English tutor and carried him to school.

We shot in a beautiful villa, located right next to my childhood home, Villa Vazir. They wanted a stylish picture of a younger me for the set so we used one from my personal collection. In fact, we used many of my own clothes because Madame Maneckshaw is supposed to be a very stylish, anglicized lady.

There were two difficult scenes in the movie. The first one was of when I walk into the sea wearing a sari. It was shot in Madh Island and four lifeguards encircled me as I walked down from the beach in case I got dragged into the current. The sari kept pooling around my feet and pulling me down as I struggled to walk gracefully into the sunset.

The other challenging scene was my funeral. I was wrapped up in white cloth, as per Zoroastrian rituals, with green make-up on my face. I had to just lie there for hours as other actors did their parts. Between shots, I would call out to the production hands and ask them to turn me to my side or scratch an itch. I couldn't even go to the loo because the wrapping was too hard to redo. To add to this ignominy, the crew forgot about me when they broke for lunch and just left me lying there!

I found the British production to be so organized. During *Sone Ka Pinjra*, we had to scrounge about for water or a place to do our make-up, but for *Sixth Happiness*, we had vanity vans, reporting and shoot timings and appointments with the wardrobe mistress.

At the end of the schedule, they wrote me a beautiful note saying they found me to be the most disciplined person who came exactly at the moment she was asked to and did exactly what she was meant to do. I don't think I did anything remarkable, but it felt nice to be appreciated.

9

Bettering Yourself

BY THE LATE '80S, I had become a household name because of my work in television. Besides kick-starting English TV programmes in India, *What's the Good Word* was the first 'edutainment' show of its kind. Because it informed and entertained, entire families would watch it together, especially children.

In the '70s and '80s, India was divided into people who spoke English correctly and fluently, and those who aspired to. Speaking the language meant sophistication, modernity, and most importantly, a pathway to advance oneself at work and in society.

Not too many people spoke English at home—only the Christians, Anglo-Indians and the Anglicized. Slowly, the generation taught by British teachers in schools was depleting and the only institutions that taught the language well were convent schools. There was no other exposure, unless you went looking for it in libraries, newspapers or the movies. TV and radio had one or two English programmes and *What's the Good Word* was the first of them. On the radio too, you would tune into a programme by the likes of Adi Marzban and hear me or Gerson da Cunha talk about creative stalwarts. And yet the Indian economy was exploding and speaking English was as crucial as computer skills are today.

With English being such a highly-valued commodity, people soon began approaching me to teach the language. In the late '80s, the Mahindras asked me to conduct a communication workshop for a group of salesmen who sold tractors in villages. They would report to the corporate offices in cities and so had double roles in that sense, having to communicate to both rural customers and urban teams.

Now, I didn't know much about tractors, let alone selling them to farmers, but what I could instruct them on was the art of gentle persuasion. I began by asking what they spoke about to their customers and found that since they were the only players in the market, the sentiment was: 'If not me, who will they buy the tractor from?'

This could be softened by communication and camaraderie. I taught the men to ask about the homes and families of their clients, and take notes in a little diary. Now they could refresh their memories before meeting their clients again. Everyone likes to be remembered and the farmers would be very touched when a chap from the city remembered the names of their children. It also mattered that they dropped their urban airs and spoke to the clients in their own lingo, mimicked their body language and shared a meal.

To communicate clearly, I told them to think about

what they were offering, in terms of pricing and after-sales service, before launching into a monologue.

It also irked me that they fidgeted with their bodies in public all the time—pulled up their pants, hands crawled into pockets and so on. I just could not resist adding a module on 'body language' to complete the course.

Then I saw them eat!

About a week after my session with them, Chotu and I were at a restaurant called Jewel of India in Nehru Centre, Worli. It was not a fine dining place but definitely one where you had to behave yourself. They were sitting at a table close to mine, and grabbing each other's knives, reaching across faces to get to the pickle while their napkins lay folded next to them. I told my husband I was going to meet them. "Surely you are not going to correct them now?" he said.

"Well, I am going to do something about it," I said, and marched over.

"Hello gentlemen," I said in a friendly way.

"Hi, ma'am. Come join us," they urged.

"No, thank you. I just happen to be with my husband; we are dining out there. But how are you eating—how are you pulling things from each other and going across people's faces...?"

"What's wrong with that?" they asked, genuinely unaware that there was anything wrong in behaving like this in public.

"Looks like I will have to come teach you some basic table manners," I said.

"That's lovely. We would really appreciate that even more than speech," they said.

And that is how my two-day module was conceived, which I called Corporate Finesse. Other companies began hearing of me, and my master manual evolved as new words crept into our vocabulary. I slowly built a reputation as a wordsmith and people would ask me to name their children, businesses or publications. I named two of my grandsons, Azhaan and Zarvaan, and the gourmet magazine *UpperCrust*.

The workshops revealed to me the common mistakes people make when speaking in public. We begin with gusto but without enough breaths, peter off at the end of sentences or simply swallow words. A master list of public speaking rules comprising even speed, eye contact, clarity and volume slowly germinated out of these workshops.

Mispronunciation is the commonest error. Unlike most Indian languages which are phonetic, English is illogical. 'Cough', 'dough' and 'bough' differ spelling wise only by one consonant, but are pronounced very differently. There are no rules to standardize spellings and pronunciation. Mispronunciations get passed around from person to person and easily normalized by repetition: for instance, our handy '*nulraj*' is a plu'mm'er not plum'b'er; and it's 'at-mus-fear' not 'at-moss-fear'. It was all the more discordant to hear young women and men talk about their 'Mount Blank' pens and 'Channel' bags.

The appropriate use and placement of articles is another common correction, because accurate usage comes through practise. We often say 'the Indian', which is incorrect, or forget that 'the' placed before a vowel is pronounced 'thee' but before a consonant is 'the'.

The workshop evolved to match India's pace of development. For instance, when I started out, there were no wines, save for the sweet port wines from Goa. Wine culture, as we know it in India, only came about in the '90s.

So, I began teaching the basics of how to inspect a wine bottle to read the name of the grape, the region it was grown in and what the year of bottling means. This extended to teaching where to place the wine glass on a table setting and how it can't be used to cool one's cheek. As foreign liquors began trickling in more freely, I put in etiquette to follow at cocktail hour, such as, not to bring your drink to the dinner table.

As corporate culture spread, there grew the need to talk about how one exchanges visiting cards, where to keep the one you have just received and how to find a way to make a small comment about the design or the person's name as a way of acknowledging it.

When cell phones became anatomical appendages, it posed quite a challenge. People had to be told to keep them aside during parties, to shut them off at interviews and meetings, and not to take calls in between meals. It's so disrespectful to cut short a conversation to answer a call and then speak loudly into the phone. I teach people to excuse themselves and take the call elsewhere, but certainly not in public bathrooms where the people in the other booths can hear you.

These sessions brought together everything I had learnt in Switzerland and from my father, and gave me an opportunity to pass them on to others. They are in demand even today and I conduct two-day sessions about twice a month all over the country. It invigorates me to see young professionals, teenagers and even retirees come to better themselves, and I always learn something new too.

More than polishing their language, participants look forward to the fine dining and corporate grooming modules, perhaps because they have more to do with personal development than a company's goals. Many come up to me and say that they felt confident interacting with their foreign counterparts or when placed in new situations after a promotion, because they knew how to handle a fork, and wear the right clothes.

In the late '80s, Mrs. Usha Batra, head of the fashion design and apparel manufacturing department at SNDT approached me to teach the students speech, diction and pronunciation as part of the personality development module. It was meant to prepare them to represent their own businesses and brands. I plunged right into it, excited to interact with a whole new group of people: keen young girls.

I was able to pour into the lessons everything I learnt about speaking on stage. A few times a week, I would request a student to sit with me to understand what the class would like to learn and what they found challenging. I would take along poems and portions of plays to class and teach the students to read them with expression and enunciation. We were all eager to play with words and would tackle homophones 'en masse' and enjoy weaving stylish phrases such as 'savoir-faire', 'au revoir', 'pied-à-terre', 'ad valorem' and 'déjà vu' into conversations.

I was as much a student as the girls: I hungered to watch them cut cloth and patterns and build a collection every year around a keyword which was presented at the end of the academic year in the fashion show called Chrysalis. Invariably, I would be roped in to compère it and would watch in wonder as the students' imagination and skill manifested on the ramp.

I also made lifelong friends at SNDT such as the designers and national treasures Wendell Rodricks and Hemant Trivedi. Wendell was a young man then, fresh from studying in Los Angeles and Paris, and taught fashion at the institute. It was Hemant's first job too, teaching fashion at SNDT, though we had met at Studio 29.

Hemant, Wendell and I became very good friends. On Hemant's 50th birthday, Wendell gifted him a Goan altar that has pride of place in his home. On it, Hemant tells me, is the Greek crucifix I got him.

I taught at SNDT for four to five years, and certainly learnt more from the students than they from me. And luckily, I met Wendell and Hemant on another leg of a similar journey.

Around the mid-'90s, when I was still teaching at SNDT, Pradeep Guha of *The Times of India* requested me to teach speech and diction to the contestants of the Miss India pageant. Aishwarya Rai and Sushmita Sen had just won international titles and the organizers realized that looking good, walking gracefully and dressing well were not enough. They needed to give the young women something internal—they had to be quick-thinking and speak well.

I was tasked with teaching the beauty queens how to take their magic beyond the footlights, exude confidence and charm the judges into seeing them as winners.

I was reunited with Hemant here, and worked closely with the then editor of *Femina*, Sathya Saran. Sathya was very incisive and discerning, and knew how to spot potential.

Hemant was driven by a passion to change the world's perception of Indian girls. He vehemently wanted to show them as erudite, confident women and shatter the stereotype of simpering, shy, downtrodden girls, so we were united on that mission. He had a feel for personality and would design with each beauty's psyche in mind and not just physical attributes. I, as a worldly woman with Indian roots, wanted to equip them to articulate their thoughts and vision for the country.

In the nascent years, all the preparatory sessions would be held in a school, usually in the far suburbs where the organizers could rent a hall or a classroom. The girls generally lodged with relatives and friends, and would travel all the way every day. By default, I would have to teach them about daily grooming and how they must now be ready to become public figures and get comfortable before the ever-present eye of the camera.

A few years later, after India made its mark as a serious contender for international crowns, the operations moved to five-star hotels. The girls were lodged two to a room, all the sessions were held in ballrooms or conference rooms, and the chef rolled out hot *nachni* rotis on the spot. With this came a panel of experts to polish these ladies to perfection: Dr. Sanjay Mayekar to bring out the perfect smile, Mickey Mehta for fitness, Dr. Jamuna Pai for skincare, and there were even meditation and art appreciation classes.

The first few batches of girls were not exposed to television or the World Wide Web. So, they would come in wanting to learn.

To prepare them for questions, the organizers and I compiled a little booklet of the most likely ones. I make them stand on the podium in that signature beauty queen pose and teach them to speak into the heart of the mike by holding it at a right angle to the mouth. Then, we fire questions, as many as 200 of them. It's always energizing to spar with a girl who is driven to better herself. If I have foreigner friends visiting, I take them to the workshop and ask them to pose a question. The intent is to familiarize the contestants with different kinds of accents as the international panel has judges from various countries.

To buy time, I tell them to use the question to formulate the beginning of the answer. Lara Dutta remembered this trick in one of the question rounds of Miss Universe when she was asked: What do you think makes women politicians different from men? "I think what makes women politicians different from men," she began, "is an amount of sensitivity." It always makes my heart jump with gratitude when they remember to do this.

The contestants also need to be reassured that it can be okay (and even charming) to admit ignorance. Many of them come from small towns and the international judges may speak in unfamiliar accents or use phrases they haven't heard before. One can simply profess, "I'm so sorry, I don't understand the meaning of this phrase. Would you please explain it to me?" No one is meant to know everything. We learn as we go through life.

Pooja Chopra, Miss India 2009, absorbed this very well and her acceptance of her vulnerability made her very likeable and approachable. She was keen on becoming the best representative of India. She thought fast, and in English, so I had to remind her to pace herself and go slow. Even today, when she is in India, she will call me up and ask if she can attend a corporate workshop or any class I am holding just to grow in confidence and refresh her skills. She says she aspires to be like me at my age, and that is the greatest compliment. She sees these skills as a means to live a meaningful and useful life, not just a stepping stone to momentary fame.

She also remembered that her behaviour off the stage mattered. In the international arena, she is not just a 'Miss India', but a representative of the country's ancient culture and modern position in the world. She was always kind and courteous, keeping in mind that whether she won the crown or not, she had to win hearts.

Sometimes, a little creativity helps one stand out. One of the Grasim Mr. Indias could not identify the talent he could demonstrate in the preliminary rounds: he didn't sing, play an instrument, write poetry, dance or juggle. We just didn't know what to do. He racked his brains and finally said, "I bake a really good sponge cake!" We gave the kitchens the batter prepared as per his recipe and when the judges asked him what his talent was, he requested some time to show them. In about 40 minutes, out came warm slices of sponge cake for the judges to taste and they were really impressed.

All this preparation leads up to the big day and contestants have to keep their wits about them. I teach them to talk themselves out of nervousness by saying, "Everybody else is more nervous than I am, and I have only that one minute to shine. So, I'll give my best and if that's not good enough, then something better is waiting for me."

I remember how Priyanka Chopra was when she came in. She is the hardest working, most committed person I have ever seen in my life. I have never come across anybody else like that—extremely focused and disciplined.

I always encourage the contestants to field questions wherever they go to practise thinking on their feet. Priyanka took it one step forward: She insisted on coming with me to SNDT on one of my teaching jaunts. "Let me listen to what the students have to say and the questions they might ask," she reasoned. "I have only had questions from older people so far."

Priyanka had been studying in America before she came to the pageant, so we had to work hard to knock off her accent. "You cannot represent India with a nasal twang," I told her, as we cultivated a neutral accent called Global English. She was driven to deliver and would read passages again and again, and ask, "Have I gotten rid of it?"

She also has innate grace and is well-brought-up. Many years later, we found ourselves on the same flight together. I was flying Economy for work, but she insisted that I come sit with her in Business Class. When I demurred, she just announced to the whole flight: "This is my ma'am. She has taught me so much. Would anyone mind if I took her to sit with me?" And the whole plane started cheering, "Go on, ma'am." I was left red-faced , yet so touched by her gesture. She was so tired that she fell asleep on my shoulder after we chatted a while.

We didn't really expect her to win, not because she wasn't deserving, but because Yukta Mookhey had won the year before in 1999 and it was unheard of to have two consecutive Miss Worlds from the same nation. When Yukta crowned Priyanka at the Millenium Dome in London, we were all wonderstruck!

Lara too has the grace to acknowledge people who were instrumental to her success, and will make her way across a crowded room to say hello to me. She was already a well-spoken, disciplined girl when she came to me, with a very well-modulated voice and excellent diction. Her greatest quality is that she thinks before answering, so there was a limited amount to do with her. We worked on expanding her vocabulary and practised answering questions.

Neha Dhupia was another driven beauty queen, which is visible in the way she has steered her career and life. She was always quick on her feet and once accompanied me on a workshop to Tata Consulting Services. I told the group to ask her a question and someone posed: "India was exporting 'tea', then it was 'beauty', then 'IT'. What is the next 'T' you think we will export?"

"Creativity," she replied without missing a beat.

Of all of us, Hemant was most certain Yukta Mookhey would win. At 5 feet 11 inches, she is one of the tallest women I know and also the most graceful. She is highly intelligent, eager to learn and aware of the world. She carried all my preparatory material from Corporate Finesse to the pageant in London, determined to keep working on herself till the very last minute. When she came back, Yukta's mother launched a personality development and grooming school to help other girls have the opportunities her daughter did.

Diana Hayden's friendly, girl-next-door demeanour could not mask her winning potential. She had an extremely approachable quality and we just had to sandpaper the edges and have her believe that she was indeed a beauty queen.

Slowly, I was approached to groom the Mr. Indias. One of them was Altamash Faraz who went on to become Mister Supranational Asia and Oceania in 2017. A lawyer by education, he has now signed on a Hindi movie. I had to remind him to not eat up his words, a skill I hope comes in handy when he recites his dialogues on screen.

At the height of the beauty queen rage, actor–filmmaker Dev Anand sought an appointment with me. He was thinking of making a film in which the protagonist aspired to become a Miss India, and wanted me to play myself—one of her mentors. He requested to sit in on a session to see how they were prepared and we were happy to have him.

He was very stylishly dressed in a blue button-down and a lemon-yellow sweater knotted at his shoulder. I don't know whether the movie ever got made, but we enjoyed having him at home.

Lately, the Miss India contest has got mired in controversy. I was told by the organizers that an international TV channel was making a documentary on the process and I agreed to be observed and interviewed. They used my bytes in the final cut, but the movie failed to show the pageant in a flattering light and the organizers were disappointed.

Of late, most of my workshops have focussed on how to do well at job interviews and I find that what I teach the Miss India contestants comes in handy here too. After all, the pageant contestant is vying for the post of the nation's beauty ambassador.

Apart from dressing appropriately and switching off the phone, one needs to speak well. This should be along the parameters of clarity, speed, volume, enunciation, pronunciation, grammar, articles, emphasis, ends of words and sentences, body language, eye contact and smile. Often, one is faced with a panel of interviewers, like the judges of a pageant. Start with the left and move to the right, acknowledging each one through eye contact.

Sometimes I have to highlight what I think is basic etiquette, but I realize with the passage of time, this has fallen out of our daily lives, such as not taking a seat at an interview until invited to or standing up when the interviewer comes in. Another soft skill is to not make the interview personal if you know the interviewer, until he takes the first step.

These days, people carry backpacks to work and not purses, so I request them to free themselves of the 'baggage' by depositing it at the reception. Purses are much easier to negotiate, and they go behind you on the chair. Sitting with legs neatly folded at an angle is a protocol the British Royals follow and a timeless morsel of elegance. The best way to remember to do all this is to arrive 20 minutes early for the appointment, collect and prepare yourself and have time to neaten up in the bathroom.

With longer, harried commutes, perky greetings such as 'Good morning' or 'Hello' are disappearing and I have to remind young folks to use them.

Like pageant judges, interviewers also find it refreshing when a potential employee is honest about not knowing something, but indicates a will to improve and move ahead. "No, I haven't worked on such a project before, but it sounds like an exciting challenge and I can apply myself," is a perfectly acceptable response.

And in the corporate jungle too, I find that all-rounders—people who have hobbies, are plugged into what's happening across the world and take the time to cultivate interests—are valued.

More than anything, Corporate Finesse gives me a purpose to wake up each morning. It allows me to take all my privileges of studying in a Swiss finishing school, my robust schooling and the world of diplomacy my father opened to me, along with the refined ways and practices of the people of South Bombay and bring it to others.

10

Friends Like Family

EVERY OTHER DAY OR SO, a postcard would arrive from Pearl. 'Dear Sebello…,' it would say, and go on to talk about how she wanted me to try a particular line on stage, or some other direction.

She would do this even if I were meeting her the same evening. In a time before mobile phones and SMSes, this was Pearl's way of instant messaging. She would buy a stack of postcards from the Indian Mail, jot down thoughts and theatre instructions as they occurred to her, and then drop them in a post box on her way to work.

Pearl Padamsee was my best friend for most of my life. We acted together in my first play *The Word*, and I was in her last one *Betrayal*. We soldiered through the trials and tribulations of life—her divorce from Alyque, her son Ranjit's battle with addiction and substance abuse, and my son Aly's descent into depression.

The first thing that struck you about Pearl was what a ball of energy she was. Once you met her, you could not forget her. Her trademark was backless cholis and saris, and she later graduated to kaftans. She taught drama at

Campion, JB Petit and a few other schools and lived in Bella Terrace on Wodehouse Road. I once met author-politician Shashi Tharoor at a party and he told me Pearl was the best teacher he ever had.

Alyque headed Lintas, and together they were the golden couple of Mumbai's intelligentsia. Were it not for my uncle Yaseen's introduction, I would not have found myself in their productions.

Their home had a peculiar layout, and recently, I bumped into the landlord, Ali Asghar, at the Yacht Club, who explained how it was made to the couple's specifications. We had to climb an almost vertical flight of wooden stairs which ended at two doors, one of which led to the apartment and the other to a large terrace that could be accessed from the home via French windows. The terrace had water tanks that could be camouflaged by sheets, and this served as a stage for our rehearsals. Raell was brought up in this world of theatre and she would run around with her nanny Rosy who made the most delicious crab curry. Rosy was like a little mother to Raell and fussed over all of us, asking what we would like to eat and taking care of our needs. Most of my evenings as a young actor were spent slogging away on this terrace in rehearsal after rehearsal.

Journalist Behram 'Busybee' Contractor who worked with *Mid-Day* then was a frequent visitor. He had a love for scotch which I developed later, and we would enjoy a drink together. Even when he spoke, it was apparent what an astute observer of human life he was. His gift for putting humanity's complexities in simple words was equally obvious. When he married Farzana, she and I became good friends.

Pearl and I bonded while I was assisting her with the costumes on *Hamlet*. I think she liked that I was organized and disciplined and not into theatre for the glamour of it. "Wouldn't it be the best thing if we were in a play together?" she said.

And soon we were. Because of her background as a teacher, she was a persuasive rather than a dictatorial director. She was so magnetic that you immediately wanted to please her. She would prase corrections diplomatically and say, "Now, shall we try this way?"

But she was also commanding. At rehearsals, she carried a little steel whistle on a string around her neck and used it with abandon. "MOVE IT" she would shout and that could mean anything—move your thoughts, your physicality while saying a dialogue, or plain "move your a**". She couldn't stand inaction of any kind.

She was also highly analytical and would get carried away while dissecting a thought. I remember coming home once to a message from her on the answering machine. But the tape ran out before she could finish her message! She called me Sebi, like Debbie, a name she made up for me.

We were together at the lowest phase of her life—her divorce from Alyque. Alyque had fallen in love with actor and news anchor Dolly Thakore, but he didn't really want to leave Pearl. The 'New Morality' he called it. Pearl had too much self-respect to go along with that—either he was wholly with her, or not at all. But she could not really get over the loss of the life she had with him, and he was never able to replace her, I think. He was her second husband and he had fought with his family and left home to marry her. She was already a divorcee with children, and Christian and Jewish parents, while he was Muslim.

Their intellectual compatibility was unmatched and he could not break the emotional bond. He would drop in often to discuss something or the other even after they split, quite unmindful of what an imposition it could be, or how painful it was for her, and she was forced into accepting this new arrangement.

Ten years and a son later, he fell in love with Sharon Prabhakar. Incidentally, Pearl had cast Sharon in a play called *Godspell* when the latter was 18. In it, Sharon sang a song called 'Day by Day'. Alyque broke the news to Dolly that he was leaving her when she was in the hospital after an accident. He just walked out of their home with his music system to marry Sharon. However, today, all of them are one happy family—Raell, Dolly and Quasar, and Sharon and Shazahn. The children doted on him and there are no more grudges or resentment between the women. I think this is testimony to Alyque's charm and magnetism.

Pearl and Alyque's divorce split the theatre crowd into two and many of our friends stopped talking to either Pearl or Alyque, because they felt they had to take sides. Though I did not approve of his ways, and didn't shun

Alyque after the incident, it was clear my loyalties lay with Pearl.

In the aftermath of this split, Pearl was consumed by taking care of her son from her first marriage to Chow (as we called him), the actor Ranjit Chowdhry, who was losing his battle with alcohol and drug addiction. The usually energetic, no-nonsense, let's-get-things-done Pearl felt hopeless and lost, but she came out of it eventually to have a second, victorious run in theatre.

Her first creative expression after the divorce came in the form of *The Serpent*. She had the marvellous idea of staging it in Scots Kirk Church (the Church of St. Andrew's) opposite Lion's Gate. She actually persuaded the pastor to allow the three actors (all women) to snake through the audience sitting in the pews, and deliver their lines from the pulpit.

All the actors wore black. I still have the dress I wore for the play and use it for my Shakespeare readings. She later directed me in *Duet for One*, my most emotionally taxing and satisfying play. Subsequently, when Raell did 'Celebrating Pearl' in 2010 to commemorate her mother's work, I enacted portions from *The Serpent*, *Betrayal* and *Duet for One*.

Chotu knew how much Pearl meant to me, and went out of his way to see to her comfort, sending over the car to ferry her to theatre rehearsals, doctor's appointments, to see Ranjit in rehab or to take him to the doctors. I still keep her picture by my bedside and say the prayer she taught us before every show:

From Strength to strength go on;
wrestle and fight and pray.
Tread all the powers of darkness down
And win your well fought day.

All the cast and crew say it while holding hands and with feeling. She was a devout Christian and I didn't know this was from a hymn until I came across it recently.

She had an intuition that *Betrayal* would be her last play. Her kidneys were failing, which made her legs swell. She wanted Gerson da Cunha to play my husband, but he looked too mature to fit the bill. So, she cast Farid Currim, who was much younger but able to look older.

She never got to see it on stage. I tried to coerce her to come to the theatre, reassuring her that I would take care of her and check on her, but her health would not allow it. Instead, she demanded a report, and I would find a phone during intervals or after the show to apprise her of what went wrong or right, and how the audience was reacting, or go meet her afterwards. She was most concerned about Farid sipping too much from his coffee mug—he put a teaspoon of rum in his black coffee before a play to deepen his voice. Pearl was quite against it, but Farid, in all these years has, never had a misstep.

Pearl loved food and I had the honour of making the last meal she had outside her house. Just a few days before she passed away, she came home for dinner, and I made a baked fillet of pomfret in a cheese sauce. She had it with a glass of red wine and we talked mainly about her health and caught up on gossip. As we saw her to the car, she waved us off with, “Darling, now don’t worry about anything. I’m fine.”

She had a black shawl with a big dramatic fringe that I had worn during a play. She insisted I take it but I kept deferring it. Today, I wish I had accepted it; I would cherish having something that belonged to her. But I know I will see her in the afterlife and we will embrace.

I missed Pearl the most as Chotu began to fade and more so when he passed away. I could have used her strength, comfort and wisdom, but God sent me Jimi instead.

Lorraine Kapur or Jimi, as we all call her, and I have been best friends for around 10 years now. We were introduced to each other at a party at Kamal Homi Mullah’s home and hit it off.

The greatest thing that binds us is our faith and belief in prayer. When Chotu passed on, Jimi would come over with sandwiches and sit with me for hours to comfort me.

I was also friends with her husband Ranjan. He was the head of O&M advertising and again, one of those people who had the most remarkable and creative brains. He passed away in January 2018 without a day’s illness and they too had a long happy marriage. So, God gave us this loss in common and we know exactly what the other is saying when we talk about our departed spouses.

Jimi is the kindest, most generous soul you could ever meet; I have never heard her say a cross word against anyone. She is also a living directory on what seems to me every person in the city, and even beyond it—she knows who married whom, who is whose sibling, what business they are in and their lineage. In the evenings at the club, we enjoy each other's company over a glass of white wine and a scotch.

In these twilight years, it's a great comfort to have a friend like Jimi, and we speak to each other nearly every day.

Another dear departed friend is Charlott Scholz. "Let's go for a beer and naan," Charlott would say the minute she landed in Mumbai bearing gifts of raclette cheese and *bündnerfleisch*—thinly sliced beef cured by crisp mountain air. She was a Swiss heiress and lived in a 13th-century home, with a door as thick as an arm, at the iconic Bahnhofstrasse neighbourhood in Zürich.

Through 20–25 years, we stayed with her for a few weeks each year. The house was a treasure trove and when she had it appraised by experts, they said the stained-glass windows were priceless. They were embedded in the walls and bore religious iconography.

Her bedroom was on the top floor, so when we reached her home (and we would have to tell her the exact time of arrival, as being Swiss, she was particular about timing), we would give a special knock and she would lower an oven mitt using a pulley with a large brass key in it to open the door. Once we went up, she would put out her palm to demand the key immediately. There was no second key, and Charlott knew that if she lost it, she would have to pay an arm and a leg to have it replicated. She eventually left her home to the city of Zürich and it is now used as a residence for the curators and directors of the city's museums.

We met because of her connection to India. In her

youth, she fell in love with an Air India pilot. Just after they announced their wedding, he went on a trip to Egypt. One ill-fated day, he was swept up by a boat's current while he was swimming, got mangled in its propeller and drowned. She never married and visited his sister and mother in Delhi every year.

She would live with us when she came to India and her trips were marked with jaunts to a small place opposite Regal Cinema for naan and beer, walks at Mahalakshmi Racecourse and a trip or two to my jeweller Hirabhai to commission something beautiful. She loved jewellery and furs and left me her exquisite chinchilla stole.

She was also a gifted cook and was able to rustle up anything with a few ingredients although she herself ate like a bird. On a trip to Mahabaleshwar, she went for a walk to the market and came back with some local greens which she washed in the sink and served with the most delicious dressing.

Charlott had the quaintest habit. She wasn't very fond of children and if coerced into hosting my grandchildren, she would ask exactly how many potatoes or what size of fish they would eat. She grew up during World War II, at a time of rationing, and had internalized the scarcity of food of those days. She always wanted to make just enough so it wasn't wasted.

She was a chemist by profession and lived life well. When we stayed with her, she would take me down to the cellar to choose the wine. We would have a white wine at lunch and a red at dinner. At 5.30–6 pm she would ring a bell and declare the bar open. Till 6.30 pm it was time for scotch, and dinner was at 8 pm where she would serve delicious veal or coq au vin.

At bedtime, she would settle in with a class of chilled champagne, adjust her bed to the right angle and dig into a crime thriller.

Uma and I are so different; it would make people wonder how we are such good friends. Our friendship dates back to school in Bandra, when she joined our gang of Jeroo Dastur, Gullu Bhagalia and Falak Naz Khan.

Uma Ghuwalewala, now Vaid, lived in Carmichael Road. I don't recall why, but instead of going to any of the fine schools in South Bombay, her parents sent her to St. Joseph's. She would motor up and down every day.

The first thing that drew me to her was that Uma was very intelligent in a way I was not—in Mathematics. She was a fun-loving girl, wearing her hair in a long bob, just as she does today. Though she participated in physical activities in school under coercion, like me, she preferred the company of a good book and that glued us together, along with a proclivity for making fun of teachers! Her brother Narain was excellent at school and since there was no one at home to help me with homework, I may have pestered him to help me with my lessons more than once.

Uma is rooted in her Rajasthani–Marwari traditions and that is where we are so different. As children, we would sit on the floor of her kitchen to eat from *thaali*s. Piping hot rotis would be dropped into our plates directly from the stove.

She still eats traditional vegetarian fare and when my daughter Heena—who loves a good *thaali*—comes down from the US, we invite ourselves over for a meal.

One deviation from her traditional ways is the fondness for scotch that Uma developed as an adult. And I am glad she did. When I was bestowed the best actress award by the All-India Critics' Association in 1981, I had to go to Calcutta to receive it, and Uma was living there then. We went to the function together, which was so cold and impersonal, but I had her to celebrate the honour with a scotch.

Besides her generosity, Uma has a very fertile green thumb. She lived in Thailand for a while when her husband Swaroop was posted there and became quite the bonsai expert. She has gifted me a few over the years and since I am no horticulturist like her, my only task has been to keep them alive.

We lost touch for a while after school, when I went to college and then abroad, but because of her geographical location, Uma was a great alibi when I began courting Chotu. She would cover up for me when I met him, saying I was with her. Of course, she had too much strength of character to ever try any stunts like that with boys herself.

Now that she is back in South Mumbai, we meet up every few months. Our friendship has progressed smoothly over all the stages of our lives. I'll make her a vegetarian baked dish when she comes over, or my mother's recipe for corn on the cob in light green coconut curry and we'll chat like the old girlfriends we are about our lives.

If there was ever a man who lived on his wit, it was Wajid Ali Khan. This hurricane of a man came into our world in the most unusual way. "Listen," said our friend and neighbour Malu Divecha, "we have a friend coming over for a few days, but I have no room to put him up. Do you think he can stay with you? He is from a very illustrious family."

"Sure," I said. Heena then had a beautiful brass bed that I had bought from an estate sale of a royal family. We decided to make up her room for the guest and bundled the kids together in one room.

Wajid Ali Khan was from the same family as the Nizams of Hyderabad. Everyone but me called him Riazudh, which was one of his names. He had broken away from the family when he was a young man and gone abroad to make his fortune, living solely on his talent. He is a striking man with a chiselled jawline, raised forehead, aquiline features and a wavy mane of hair that was greying at the temples. He wore sharp suits and was the epitome of European charm.

Nothing could prepare you for the force of his personality—he was effusively grateful for our hospitality and lavishly French in manners. "What have we got ourselves into!" Chotu and I said to each other as he threw our household into a spin with his enthusiasm.

However, he and Chotu formed a close friendship soon. He was full of stories of nobility and jokes, and once he sat down at a table, you were sure to be entertained.

Wajid made his living by dealing in precious stones. He would procure near-perfect rocks dismantled from the ornaments of royalty by the likes of Harry Winston or Cartier, and find them new lovers. His clientele was made up almost exclusively of aristocrats, and he counted Prince Rainier, Harry Winston and Gianni 'Johnny' Bulgari among his friends.

Wajid being Wajid had the peculiar habit of carrying these gemstones on his person. As we got to know him better, we realized that it was perfectly normal for him to carry a flawless Golconda diamond in this blazer, or slip a fistful of Ceylon sapphires in the special hidden pockets of his bespoke swimming trunks. He would then produce them for a count or countess to examine in the most cavalier approach to business.

I guess he had realized that the safest place for them was on his person, but this did lead to a few near-heart attacks. Once, he thought he had misplaced an eight-carat Columbian emerald, only to find it nearly a year later in the breast pocket of a dinner jacket.

Another time, he bought four- to five-carat Burmese rubies from Harry Winston and then stepped out to lunch with him. When he came back to Harry's office, an assistant handed him the pouch that held the gems. He had dropped it in the elevator without realizing it, but luckily, Harry's secretary stepped into it soon after and found them on the floor.

Given his last name, he was often mistaken for one of the Aly Khans, the spiritual leader of the Ismaili Muslims. And Wajid never corrected this assumption. It got him many a reservation at tony hotels and excellent service!

Another time, we were in Las Vegas with our friends Tikam and Nirmala Chulani (or Dada and Didi as we called them). Heena and I were relaxing in a bubble bath upstairs when the telephone rang. "Mrs. Merchant!" boomed a voice on the other end of the line. "You have won one million dollars. Please come down to the casino at once."

I was so excited! We went down and sat at the Blackjack table where Chotu was betting. After a short while, I felt something sharp behind my ear and a voice said, "Stick 'em up! Give me all you got!" I panicked, only to turn around and see it was Wajid. He was in Las Vegas too and when he found out we were around, he joined us on our holiday.

Now, Wajid was a cultivated European and not familiar with American etiquette. When we sat down to breakfast in Las Vegas, he gestured to the waitress and said, "I would like a mimosa, please."

"There's the champagne and there's the OJ," she said in a thick nasal accent, motioning towards the buffet table, "Go get it ya self."

"But I wish to be served," he said, incredulously. We were all stunned. He was used to the finesse of fine establishments such as Perle du Lac, his favourite restaurant in Geneva, not the efficiency and self-help culture of the country that conceived McDonald's.

When we met Wajid, he was married to his first wife Inge with whom he had four children. Then one day, while he was shopping, he spotted Elizabeth Schar in the store across the road and fell in love instantly.

Elizabeth was a striking, tall, lithe, blonde Estonian. She was so beautiful that her mother feared for her. She was a furrier by profession, employed by one of the most elite stores in Geneva. She accepted Wajid's advances and he divorced his first wife to marry her. Together, they have a daughter Leila, who recently married a member of the Russian royal family.

Wajid's profession could not guarantee them a steady living—he would be flush after the sale of a stone and then there would be long periods of drought. So, Elizabeth opened a chocolaterie called Chocolaterie de Mont Blanc on the main avenue encircling Lake Geneva and worked very hard to support the family.

Competition in the chocolate business is predictably tough in Switzerland but Elizabeth built up a clientele on the strength of her warmth. She would always chat with the patrons, remember their names, ask about their families and make the encounter in her store more than a mere transaction.

Elizabeth and I cultivated a close friendship nourished by many meals of rösti and bratwurst. Her mother, 'mamma' as we also called her, visited us once in Mumbai. Whenever we left the Ali Khans' home, she would see us to the door and immediately sweep the foyer. This peculiar habit was a traditional Estonian goodbye. It indicated that the dust would be swept back into the house by our next visit.

Elizabeth also has the two qualities present in all my close friends—warmth and generosity. One unforgettable gift from her was a holiday in Yvoire, an island in Lake Geneva. She booked us into the best room overlooking the waterfront. We also took many holidays together, travelling to Paris, Amsterdam, Annecy and other places.

Given her expertise, it was also Elizabeth I turned to when I wanted to buy a mink coat in the 1980s. It was impossibly glamorous at the time to own one and I asked her to help me choose it.

Instead of a shop, she advised that I go directly to a furrier. "You want one made just for you," was her advice. She helped me choose the right pelt, fussing over the length of the hair, its density and the matching of the colour gradation. For my stature, she suggested a cropped jacket with slightly raised sleeves at the shoulder and clasped at the wrist. We had one made, which I store in a fur vault in New York.

A constant on our home menu is a red Mangalorean curry we call 'Amma's curry'. That and the white Husain hanging in our living room is the legacy of my friend Malu Divecha.

Malu and I were young mothers who matured as parents together since my son Aly and her son Arjun were the same age. We would see each other almost every week for a movie at the Cambatas' preview theatre or a potluck meal at someone's place.

Malu was a pottery artist, and had a studio with a kiln above her apartment in Altamount Road. She also conducted ceramic art classes for children. She was also a terrific and audacious cook, conjuring sizzlers and overseeing barbecues at her home, not to mention lip-smacking soups, prawn samosas, and delicacies of the South.

When she started cookery classes, I sent our chef Vasu (who is still with us, after some 40-odd years) to learn from her. He came back with copious notes in English, which I then read out to him as he wrote them down in Malayalam. Amma's curry, with *neer* dosa, came to us through Vasu's term with her, as did *paniyaram*s.

Malu was a tall dusky woman, always in bright *mul* or silk saris with a large *bindi*. She graduated to kaftans as she grew older, and was a real people person. Bhagwan and she had a strong marriage and he was an indulgent husband. When he passed away, at barely 60, she amped up her social life. One of her final dreams was to publish a cookbook, which she did. And on the cover was a picture of her in a bikini!

When she couldn't cook for her friends anymore, Malu began to throw 'dosa parties'. A dosa 'chef' in the balcony would flip different kinds of dosas and the table was laden with curries, chutneys and coconut rice.

She got her flair for cooking from her mother who lived on Lamington Road. The kitchen in her maternal home had a stone masala grinder, the kind that needs a few people to carry into the house and then can never be moved! She would grind her masalas with a stone pestle, with everyone in the house giving it a go to share the labour. We used mixies, of course, but it never tasted the same.

Bhagwan had a huge room in their home devoted to model racing cars. He had an intricate track built that looped through the room and Russi (Cambata), Ranjan, Chotu and Bhagwan would spend hours there racing cars together.

Malu was generous about everything—her talents, her time, her contacts. She wasn't secretive or possessive. The moment you told her you liked a dish, she would tell you how to make it. When sizzlers became all the rage, she made us a set of sizzler plates that we still have. In the late '70s, she made a wall hanging of 12 faces of the sun—ceramic plates that represented the sun through emotions and colours. She gifted it to me as a room divider. If she became friendly with an artist whose work she thought resonate with you, she would connect the both of you over a sequence of dinners. That is how we became friends with Jehangir Sabavala; we own two of his works. She also cared for her unmarried sister Prema who was always a part of our outings and evenings.

Since Malu was also artistic, we became gallery and play buddies, repairing to Samovar for prawn curry after we had checked out who was showing at the Jehangir Art Gallery. She also introduced me to gallerist Kali Pundole, who was more concerned with finding a painting a home with those who understood and enjoyed it, rather than just selling it to anyone.

It was a time when artists such as Laxman Shrestha,

VS Gaitonde, Shanti Dave and Adi Davierwalla were making their mark, and when Kali came across a work he knew would resonate with me, he would ring up to urge, "*Aa tu levuch jooyye* (You must buy this)." If I told him that I didn't have the money, "*Paisa tu* instalment *ma aap ni* (Pay me in instalments)," he would say. And that is how I built an art collection out of my household budget with each piece costing only a few thousand rupees then. It has now become a sizeable legacy.

One day in the '70s, Malu came to me and said that there was this painting by MF Husain that I must go see right away. We went landed at Pundole Art Gallery and sure enough, there was a painting of white horses that just arrested my attention. But the price tag said ₹7,000! I didn't have that kind of money. This was the time when I ran the house on ₹3,000 every month and meat cost ₹1.25 paisa a kilo!

I asked whether I could pay in bits, and it took a few months of shaving off money from the household budget and my savings to finally own it.

When a few years later, Doordarshan produced a documentary on Husain, I suggested both of us sit on the sofa under this painting, browse through a book on his work and talk about his method and inspirations.

We did that and then there was a shot of him walking up and down a gallery with a lantern. "This is how inspiration comes to me," he said. "Like light from a lantern and then I have to brush it down."

We also wanted to shoot him in Mohammed Ali Road, going to the masjid to offer Friday prayers. The camera crew and I were following him on an oppressively sultry day, when a young woman raised the flap of her burqa, giving us a glimpse of her beautiful face.

Husain spun on his heels and said, "*Bas. Aaj kuch* shooting *nahin hogi. Mujhe usske saath jana hai*! (That's it. No shooting today. I have to follow her!)"

I ran after him, pleading, "*Aap aisa nahin kar sakte. Pura* crew *hai*! (You can't do this. We have hired a crew!)", but there was no stopping him.

Since we didn't have footage to show for the day, DD refused to pay the crew and I ended up paying them. The documentary was also shelved since it was incomplete.

Husain was a shade remorseful about this, and whenever he met me, he would say, "I let you down that one time." "Yes, you did," would be my standard reply.

I wonder whether DD still has footage from the documentary in the archives. It would be invaluable material.

I would still bump into the legendary artist when he came to Darshan Apartments (where I live) to meet his friend Bal Chhabra on the seventh floor. He would emerge from a taxi and if he saw me walking in the lawns or running an errand, he would beckon me to say, "Taxi *ka paisa de do* (Pay the cabbie)," turning out his pockets to show he had no money.

He was authentically a bohemian fakir, and never carried cash. If he was hungry, he would simply join someone for a meal saying, "*Main aap ke saath khaana khata hu* (I am eating with you)."

"Now what would you do if you hadn't met me, or I didn't have any cash," I reprimanded him once. "I would just walk away," he shrugged. "What can people do?"

11

How I Awakened Spiritually

AT THE AGE OF 60, I renewed my bond with my maker and forged a relationship that has brought me immense peace and purpose. Funnily, I was always a spiritual and religious person even though Daddy was strictly a token Muslim, praying only on holy days for Dadima's benefit and rarely going to a mosque. Chotu was even less ritualistic. What both men took from Islam was the message of peace, goodwill and brotherhood towards all men.

So varied is our household that neither our children, their spouses, nor our grandchildren are Muslim, and I only realized the fact while writing this book!

I've always sought a bond with a higher power, which must come from Bapaji. In Bandra, I was ensconced in the fellowship of Christianity—the prayers in our school, the peaceful face of Christ Our Redeemer, helping my neighbours make *kulkuls* and marzipan sweets at Christmas and Easter, etc. In all the faiths around me—our Parsi friends and Hindu relatives—I saw a close and loving relationship with God.

While growing up, I was a dutiful Muslim, performing the namaz daily and keeping *rozas*. I could feel God's invisible hand guide my life to reach my full potential: my adoption, the love of my two fathers, staying back in India, and then arranging my meeting with my soulmate and helping me lead a fulfilling life. How could I not feel divine love? But a series of events when I was in my 60s led to a deeper spiritual awakening.

I had gone to Africa with some ladies from the club, and I started feeling ill there. There was a knot in the centre of my stomach and I didn't want to look at food at all. The doctor said it was my gallbladder. "It has enlarged to about seven times its size, and food is not being digested," he said. "We have to remove it surgically," he added.

I underwent laparoscopic surgery to remove the organ, but it being a keyhole surgery, the surgeon didn't notice that the bile duct leading to it had narrowed. So I was in agony even after the operation. The bile duct had also gone into a kind of shock, and the doctors said they would have to go in again to open the vein.

I had to undergo endoscopy five times and even consulted various specialists in New York. Finally, I landed up in Adelaide, New Zealand, on the examining table of the best surgeon in the field. He recommended inserting a stent into the passage to enlarge the duct. But I was in agony even after that and kept dropping kilos because I could eat very little without bringing it back up.

It seemed like the end of the road, and both Chotu and I were disheartened. "I don't know where to go now," my husband said as we sat on the sofa in our home. "What do we do next? You are in so much misery..."

Just then, the bell rang. It was our friends Sheila and Gul Kriplani. "We felt like coming to say hello, to see how you were feeling..." they said.

"I'm okay but in a lot of pain," I replied. As we sat with a drink, Chotu, out of the blue, asked, "Will you pray for her?" This surprised me as he was not a pious man.

"Actually," they said, looking at each other, "we came in wanting to pray for Sabi, but didn't want to impose..."

They shut their eyes, held my hand and started praying earnestly, beseeching the Almighty to heal me. I experienced a sudden movement within like the pain was being pushed out of my body by a growing sphere of light. The next morning, when I went for a check-up, the doctor was shocked to see that the stent had popped out. "It's floating! This means I have to go in once more to remove it, but no more stents," he said.

While I was undergoing that surgery, again, I experienced a sudden surge of light within me and then total darkness. The pain just vanished, and in its place was the awareness of an awakening. It felt as if somebody had just turned the lights off, and for years I was suffering. And now, there was this release.

Very swiftly, I weaned off the medication and began to eat and drink normally.

When I felt better, in my mind's eye, I took a whole

bundle of worries and flung it at God's feet. "You do what you want with it," I said.

After this episode, a higher spirit came like a force to me. Once, I even passed out while praying but felt as if I were floating on a cloud. Many books that I have read describe this experience as being open to divinity and the spirit of consciousness entering one's body. When that happens, you lose sense of this world and are transported to another plane where there is no fear. You are not contained by your body, gender or location. When I came back to this world, I found myself on my sofa.

Since then, the umbilical cord connecting me to a higher power has become more of a direct line with a longstanding pal. Christ and I are always talking. My days begin and end with prayer, and I intervene on behalf of my friends. "Let's talk about XYZ," I'll tell Christ when they are troubled, "You have to make her better."

Chotu saw a change in me too. While it was always in my nature to be kind, I was no longer interested in the self as much as I was in others. I went out of my way to do things for people, to pray for them, inquire about their health, to sit with them and comfort them. I became charitable not only of money but also of time.

Chotu, who was totally irreligious, decided to follow Christ too a few years after my baptism. "Don't do it because of me. Do it for your own self," I told him. "I wish it, I feel it," said Chotu. "It's an inner calling." So he joined me in Christianity and we had a good laugh about being the oldest people to be baptized.

We faithfully began going to church together— me a few times a week and Chotu on Sundays. We would also pray at home with each other. As we made plans for end days, Chotu expressed his wish to be buried with me. He requested a cremation and his ashes are in an urn that will go into my grave.

I shall be ever grateful to Sheila and Gul for bringing me to the Lord. The All Saints Church on Malabar Hill has become my second home and sanctuary. I pop into it few times a week— for a prayer, to lay my worries at Christ's feet or for a quick catch-up with him. Especially on the days I miss Chotu, I go there and ask the Lord to take my pain away.

During the lockdowns enforced by the global Covid-19 pandemic, Christianity gave me a grounding ritual that brought me a great sense of peace. It was the daily prayer meeting held by the Spark Family at 7 pm, that terribly lonely hour before dinner which I would have usually spent chatting with Chotu or with family.

It was a new group with members we had never met before, yet we ended up knowing each other so well through this path. Pastors from all over the world would speak and it gave me a great sense of purpose to listen to them and take part in the prayers.

In the end, all religions are a path to find peace within yourself, no matter the circumstances around you. It should end the questioning and ever-churning turmoil in your mind and replace it with total acceptance and peace.

I am no longer afraid to sleep alone at home because I know I am under divine protection. And most often, I hold God to his promise: A peaceful death to match this wonderful life.

12

I Live the Life I Teach

EVERY MORNING, I WAKE up to a packed calendar of exercise, play readings, social engagements, home maintenance, prayer meetings and etiquette workshops. I am not ready for the box yet, though I am prudent enough to not buy green bananas.

I still have my sunny outlook, bolstered by faith. I lost Chotu in December 2016 and my firstborn, Aly, two months later in February 2017. I allow myself to grieve for them and honour their memory, but don't revel in it. I compel myself to see this too as a gift: God arranged for my last years to be unfettered.

Over the past decade or so, as Chotu's health deteriorated, he became increasingly housebound, and I devoted my energies to his care. Yet, I never gave up the daily rituals or activities that nourish me, nor did I cut down on work. I was still doing theatre, conducting self-improvement workshops and training the Miss Indias. I just learned to fit it all in and I was able to do this by pre-empting what could go wrong.

I held on to my intent to live a full life because I didn't want to resent anything; nor did I want Chotu to feel guilty that 'Sabi did not do this or that because of me'. It would have changed our relationship. We would call each other every two hours to check in. "I am fine," he would say. "Don't worry about me. Take your time. Do your workshops." Thus we remained lovers and friends till the very last day.

To fit everything in, I just organized better, delegated adequately, planned ahead and made a timetable. I would discuss Chotu's medication and physical therapies with the brother (nurse) every morning.

As his health deteriorated and he had to use a wheelchair, Chotu found it hard to make the effort to go out, though he always felt better when he came back. So, I would start warming him up for the outing by discussing what he would like to wear at the beginning of the week, giving him choices of outfits. Then I would keep dropping lures such as, "Oh, I hope we meet so-and-so on Wednesday evening. You would love to hear about their trip to Croatia," to keep the evening on the radar and get him excited. Then on the day itself, I would remind him every hour: "We'll have a small drink at home and have an actual one when we get there..." or start sentences with, "When we go out..."

After Chotu passed away, sticking to my routine kept me afloat. I still get to the breakfast table in full make-up and dressed for the day. I keep my first appointment for 11 am. When I come back from a social evening, I speak to Chotu as if he is still there, tell him about what someone said, or the music and food. My table is still set for dinner with candles because I cannot let myself sink into despondency; that is not what he would have liked.

The main pillar of my active life is my daily exercise, which I never compromise on because I know how good it makes me feel. I also know it needs to be regular to be effective; it's not a pill you pop once a week. Sometimes, I even split it into two batches of 40 minutes on the treadmill while I read a newspaper, and another hour of functional training later.

When we went into a lockdown in 2020, and again in 2021 because of the Covid-19 pandemic, I still did not miss a single day's workout. We just moved our sessions to video call in the evening, which I followed up with a walk in the garden in our apartment complex.

The most important aspect is that I work with a personal trainer. Otherwise, it's easy to give in to an ache or a lazy day. Working with a young man also opens up his world to me. We talk about the latest in fitness and wellness, his family and life. It takes me into a world beyond my Malabar Hill and seniors-at-the-club existence, which is crucial to keep abreast of the times.

Beautification of the house is an ongoing process, along with the sorting of things to give away. If I let the apartment wither, it will stop being our home.

Evenings are for spending with my friends or at the club if I am not at the occasional rehearsal. I would like to do more theatre, but frankly, the roles are drying up. Even if I don't look it, I have been on stage for more than half a century and everyone in the world of theatre knows that. But I still don't pass up on an opportunity to play a part or do a reading because I like to keep my brain agile by memorizing lines.

When I catch up with my friends, I have a rule: No talk about body parts, please. If we are not careful, it starts with an aching knee, and before you know it, we are all morosely celebrating and revelling in our deteriorating joints and cosseting our weak hearts and digestion. I even go a step further and prepare for the direction I want to steer the conversation in. Usually, I'll pick something I have read in the newspaper: the elections, the stock market, an author or a book. If you were interested in these topics at 40, why should you lose interest in them at 60?

During the pandemic-imposed lockdowns, I got closer to another circle of friends; and we call ourselves Durga's Club in honour of Durga Chulani who brought us together. We have all lost our husbands and our group on WhatsApp is the liveliest one on my phone. Besides Durga and my BFF Jimmi, there is Rekha Tanna and Sudha Motwani.

Rekha lives close to me and I can drop into her house anytime I am lonely. She is a Rotarian too, and is a great organiser. She had managed our trip to Korea a couple of years ago, and helped me and staff all get vaccinated against Corona. She takes great care of me. Bouts of vertigo have sent me reeling recently, and she is very vigilant about giving me a hand lest I go off balance when we are walking.

Chotu and I were friends with Sudha and her husband Giddu, but the two of us have gotten closer in the lockdown. She lives in Khar and we went to the Willingdon Club regularly in the brief months that the lockdown was lifted, to pass the evening together.

Durga is a very feisty 85 year old who lives on Napean Sea Road. She is very warm and we bond over our love for caviar. "I have some caviar in the freezer," she will call to say. "Why don't you come over. We'll pop open some champagne and forget about the lockdown." I'm glad to be around someone so positive.

After Alyque passed in 2018, I missed having someone to gab about any old thing. But Sabi's Boys, as they call themselves, keep me in touch in with theatre. That's Nishit Dhanak, Farid Currim and Rayo Noble. Before the lockdown, we would get together about once a month at my home for dinner. Each would bring a dish with him and we would have some drinks and discuss what's happening on stage.

Before the lockdown, I would travel a lot more because it took my grief away. Time really is a healer even though you don't want to believe it when you are in the throes of sorrow. I take trips with the ladies of my club and other friends, and go see my family in New York. Just as I did with my husband, I stay in a hotel close by, preferring to keep my independence. My grandchildren visit me as often as they can, as does my daughter. Saleem, who lives close by at Breach Candy, really stepped into Chotu's shoes during the pandemic, taking care of my every need.

He and Tayunaz were the only ones physically close to me, and they took all responsibility for my well-being. Tayunaz and her mother Katy would call me up often to check if I needed anything, while Saleem keeps an eye on my financial matters. He also supervises everything that needs to be done at home—small repairs, installation of new equipment, etc. He would call the workmen each time and remind them to wash their hands and sanitize everything before entering my home. He pushes me to meet people in my building, and so that I wasn't isolated!

I still pay attention to my appearance and am always reading about medical advances. When people exclaim that I don't look my age, I tell them unabashedly that I do many, many things to look the way I do. However, I would not impose on anyone and tell them what to do. I am happy to give advice if asked but baulk at the thought of pointing out that someone's hair is thinning and what he can do about it.

I enjoy dressing up and pursuing beauty; I see it as a mark of respect to myself and to the people I meet. At my age, many of my friends have lost loved ones and seen tragedies. A long, drawn face is the last thing I want to subject them to when we meet. "My! Aren't we glamorous," Gerson remarked once when we met for a reading. And I was quite pleased about it.

Even during the lockdown, my pajamas were strictly for bedtime. Never did I loll about in a kaftan or get lazy about my appearance, never mind that I had nowhere to go and no one to see. I would still dress up and have my make-up on before I sat down for breakfast, and kept up my ritual scotch before dinner and wine with food. I simply did not allow myself to slide into ennui.

I push myself harder and take up little projects that keep me alert: colouring books, an engagement party for my grandson and his fiancée, never passing up an opportunity to meet new people.

In fact, I spent the pandemic teaching and learning. My classes on etiquette and diction reached a larger audience through the online Master Classes organised by Celebrity School. Besides those that I personally mentor, I spent much of my time polishing Miss Diva Universe 2020 Aldine Castelino for the Miss Universe pageant in Miami. We practised diction by reading out lines from plays and I was very satisfied with my hard work when she came out of herself and began projecting her voice and personality. Like all of us, I learnt to use Zoom and other apps on my phone and laptop. A very clever young lady called Sonal Sanghvi would teach me how to use these a few times a week.

In September 2019, just before the world was shut down by the Covid-19 pandemic, our family got together in New York for one of the most joyous moments of my life: The wedding of my eldest grandson Arjun to Annie. He is the first among my six children to get married, and I enjoyed planning and preparing for the event months in advance because I wanted everything to be perfect.

Morbidity and despondency would defile this glorious life I have been given. I have tasted true, everlasting love and friendship, raised my children who are now my soulmates and guardians, put to use all the gifts God gave me and, hopefully, honoured the memory of my fathers. I have been given opportunities to see different worlds and be different people. And at life's every turn, I have been met by the kindness of strangers.

Acknowledgements

THIS BOOK OWES A debt of gratitude to a serpentine line of people that stretches back to the 1950s and 60s. First of all, to Daddy and Bapaji—who gave me the roots and the freedom to grow as God intended.

Alyque's kind words came just a few days before he moved on to the larger stage. Pearl, who is gone but never forgotten—I miss you every day. My 'fourth child' Raell, who honours and deepens the bond forged with her parents.

To Gerson da Cunha, Roger Pereira, Kabir Bedi, Vijay Crishna, Farid Currim, Dalip Tahil and Nikki Bedi who graciously agreed to share what transpired in the wings.

My gratitude to the Studio 29 gang—Phiroze Vazifdar, Sangeeta Chopra, Rukshana Eisa, Kailash and Aarti Surendranath—who keep its spirit alive. The dates and details of the period would not have been possible without the elephantine memory of my then secretary Wilma Rego.

Jimi, Uma, Shirley and Katayun, thank you for keeping our girlhood alive.

Pinning down all these important dates would not have been possible without my son Saleem's impeccable memory and my daughter Heena's eagle eye for detail. Aly was sorely missed on this trip down memory lane. Dhananjay and Tayunaz, you are immeasurable gifts to this family. Thank you, Saleem Bhai, for always tethering me to my blood family though we are countries apart. To Monica Vaziralli for nurturing our relationship beyond formal ties.

Thank you, Reena Jayswal, the commissioning editor from Jaico Publishing House, for her relentless care while steering this book all the way and for introducing me to Mitali Parekh, whose help has been unlimited.

Beyond everything and everyone else, I would like to thank my children Aly, Heena and Saleem for sharing their mother with the world all their lives.